HOW TO GET ALONG WITH ANYONE

63 Strategies for Success

Susan Mendoza Beller, JD, LLM

ISBN-13: 978-0615905037
ISBN-10: 061590503X

Library of Congress Control Number: 2013919836
RecipeForPeaceNow Publishing, Washington, DC

Publishing Agent: R.C. Prentiss
Acquisitions Editor: S. Morton
Developmental Editor: M.A. Cunningham
Project Manager: S. Stanton

To my wonderful Mother,
the most important person in my life.

CONTENTS

DEDICATION

Phil Smart, Sr., (1919-2013)

This book is dedicated to the memory of my friend and mentor Phil Smart who was the guiding light for RecipeForPeaceNow (www.recipeforpeacenow.com).

Phil taught me that: "We are aware of eight areas of true social pain infecting every village, town and metropolis in our world: the Hurt, the Hungry, the Homeless, the Unemployed, the Young, the Old, the Illiterate and the Drugged. Where do we as people, as a nation find help, a healing, a cure? Perhaps we turn to the one I know best: Me.

I realize that I am blessed, like everyone in the world, with twenty-four precious hours each day; life to death. Most of us spend eight hours in school, at work, or retirement. We spend a second eight hours at rest, preparing for tomorrow.

What happens to the balance, those discretionary third eight hours given us to spend as we see fit? If we are now aware of opportunities to share ourselves, where does it begin?

This question begs for a logical and believable answer. Perhaps it is this: If we gather together, nation upon nation, beginning with our own and become personally involved in a specific area of pain, we might, one-to-one, change the world! This action begins with whom? Me!"

INTRODUCTION

Whenever I facilitate a mediation or other type of alternative dispute resolution, conduct a seminar, teach a class, hold a workshop, or make a speech, people always ask: "How do you know what people are thinking, and how they will react?"

The purpose of this book is to provide a better response than: "I've been practicing for over thirty years … I just know." I have been incredibly honored, gratified and amazed by the outpouring of support for RecipeForPeaceNow (www.recipeforpeacenow.com) — the global peace through mediation project that I founded in 2010. This book would not have been possible without the life-lessons taught by our wonderful participants. Because of them, I've learned that people all over the world sincerely strive to understand each other, and desperately want to be understood.

During my three decades of working with groups needing change, I've learned that "making these ideas our own" happens with practice. I have seen and experienced just about every type of team-building activity, and I favor those games that are non-exclusionary, require little physical dexterity, and have simple instructions requiring no special equipment. Competitive activities create winners and losers. Nobody wants to be on the losing team. The sole purpose of all of the activities is to foster a shift in our interpersonal communication and listening skills. There are no losers because everybody wins.

Large groups will need to be divided into smaller teams for the activities. I use different colored LEGO pieces, one for each participant in evenly divided colors, placed in a large bowl. Participants select a color that designates their team for the day. If the group meets regularly, participants are required to choose different colors each meeting to create interaction with everyone. It's easy and fun to lead a successful activity when leaders bring genuine enthusiasm, set reasonable time limits, and remember to be flexible in encouraging positive participant response.

This book is not intended to provide a blueprint for dealing with other people. Humans are complex creatures. In real life, there is a substantial amount of crossover between the various strategies, examples and activities. This book is intended to be a starting point for reflection, analysis and understanding.

John Steinbeck wrote: "Your audience is one single reader. I have found that sometimes it helps to pick out one person — a real person you know, or an imagined person — and write to that one." Thank you for being my reader.

DISCLAIMER

Fewer things are harder to put up with than the annoyance of a good example. ~ Mark Twain

All examples are composites developed over three decades of being a practicing business lawyer and professional mediator. Therefore, if you have been my client, and you absolutely, positively, recognize yourself as the antagonist in one of the examples…you're mistaken!

LET'S GET STARTED

When confronted with two courses of action, I jot down on a piece of paper all the arguments in favor of each one, then on the opposite side, I write the arguments against each one. Then by weighing the arguments pro and con and cancelling them out, one against the other, I take the course indicated by what remains. ~ Benjamin Franklin

In *How To Get Along With Anyone: 63 Strategies For Success* we will approach and use only those tools that problem-solve and enable negotiated compromise. Using approaches from psychology, philosophy, science, and even mythology, we will be able to successfully understand and deal with all types of personalities in potential conflict. We do not need to solve deep-seated psychosis. That's not our goal. The goal is to create workable solutions no matter what type of person we're dealing with. The goal is to to recognize the issues and find the right solution before the situation careens out of control.

ONE

ACHILLES HEEL

"Everyone is a moon and has a dark side which he never shows to anybody." ~ Mark Twain

In ancient Greek drama, the mythical hero in the Trojan War was Achilles. He was a demi-god — immortal, but with one important area of vulnerability. He could be killed as a mortal man if struck on the heel of his foot. Of course, according to Homer's epic poem *The Iliad*, Paris kills Achilles by shooting an arrow into his heel. Paris knew about the vulnerability and used it to his tactical advantage. Even a mythical hero has his weakness.

We all have an area of vulnerability. Everyone has a topic, behavior, or "pet peeve" that elicits an exaggerated and unreasonable response, especially in the workplace.

EXAMPLE:

Conrad was always professionally polite to his colleagues, friendly without over-stepping personal boundaries, and basically even-tempered. He had opinions, some of them very definite, but he never forced his ideas on anyone else, and he never proselytized. He considered discussing personal opinions to be inappropriate workplace behavior. However, Conrad did have his own "Achilles Heel," a topic that annoyed him so much that he flew into a rage whenever it was brought up for even casual discussion.

The sensitive topic was politics in Germany during the Nazi era. Conrad was sensitive because his beloved wife, and her entire family, had been forced to flee the region due to political and religious disagreement with the Nazi regime. His wife had been an infant when her family left Germany, and the directly influenced adult family members were all dead, but both Conrad and his wife deeply resented her family trauma as though it had happened yesterday. His coworkers didn't realize his sensitivity until one day, during lunch, the discussion turned to a recently shown public television documentary examining Hitler's rise to power. Everyone in the office had seen it, and they all agreed that it was both informative and interesting.

Conrad flew into a rage. He accused his co-workers of favoring the Nazi government and acting as spies against the German people. He aggressively sprang to his feet in the middle of the employee lunchroom, sang the German National Anthem, and publicly declared them no longer his friends because of their "insults."

His co-workers were shocked. None of them had even visited Germany, and they did not know Conrad well enough to know his wife or her family. They had not meant to be insulting, and they certainly were not spies against the German people. They were merely discussing a PBS documentary. Still, Conrad left the building in a rage. He called his wife to tell her what had happened at work.

His wife was shocked and embarrassed by his outburst. She realized that his coworkers had no reason to know of his personal sensitivity. They were innocently discussing a movie. His wife gently reasoned with him, and Conrad calmed down.

Conrad immediately realized that his response had been unwarranted. He went back to the lunchroom, explained his personal situation, and publicly apologized. Everyone was happy to accept his apology. They never discussed Germany, or the Nazis, again.

STRATEGIES FOR SUCCESS:

Conrad recognized his mistake, after his wife pointed it out and "talked him down," and was able to successfully apologize. He had overreacted, but he hadn't done anything so egregious that it was beyond forgiveness. To prevent overreaction, and the potential for serious professional relationship harm, privately recognize, and consciously acknowledge, areas of vulnerability. When your personal vulnerability is violated, refuse to succumb. Recognize personal vulnerability in others, and refuse to exploit it. When someone else exhibits their "Achilles Heel," always accept a sincere apology.

DIALOGUE ACTIVITY:

Setting a reasonable time limit for each response, have each person in the group select and answer an open-ended question selected from a written choice of questions. Open-ended questions are those that begin with "what," "where," "when," "how," and "why." When we engage in these dialogue activities, we practice responding to questions, listening to answers, and developing understanding that will prevent stepping on some-one's "Achilles Heel."

DISCUSSION IDEAS:

Did we learn something interesting about everyone in the group? Which question was the most popular? Were there similarities between the answers?

TWO

ARISTOTLE'S ETHICS RULE

"I count him braver who overcomes his desires than him who conquers his enemies, the hardest victory is the victory over self." ~ Aristotle

Aristotle's basic "ethics rule" is that there is no list of rules. Aristotle philosophized that being ethical is simply a matter of character development. He thought that when humans practice virtuous acts, being virtuous becomes a habit. This habit then develops into a desirable character trait.

The contemporary science of "virtue ethics" was developed using Aristotle's foundational premise: When we think about "virtue," we often envision a religious connotation. However, according to Aristotle and contemporary definitions developed by modern "virtue ethics," virtue is not a religious concept. Virtue is the "mean" or "the golden middle" between the extremes of good and bad. Virtue is the "mean" between "excess" and "deficiency." For example, the virtue of courage lies between the excess of foolhardy daring and the deficiency of cowardice.

EXAMPLE:

Isabella considered herself to be a person of good character. Numerous awards and plaques on her office walls attested to her good works. She generously donated money to charitable organizations, coached Girl Scouts, and was a considerate neighbor. She was certain that she was personally virtuous. Unfortunately, her job required a certain amount of ethical flexibility in order to be successful. Isabella was very successful.

Isabella was a professional financial planner. She did whatever needed to be done to make money for herself and her clients. She "bent" the government rules and regulations regarding financial and fiduciary responsibility. She could handle it. She was a stock market expert. She knew what she was doing. The rules and regulations were for stupid novices. They didn't apply to her. The more financially successful she was, the further she "bent" the rules. She enjoyed the challenge, and her clients enjoyed the high percentage earnings. Her reputation, and her client portfolio, impressively increased every year.

Isabella habitually chose high-yield, high risk, investments. The amount of debt was substantially greater than the amount of available funds. She didn't disclose the risky nature of these investments, even though "full disclosure" was legally required. Clients would only worry about their money and ask too many questions. She decided clients didn't need to worry; they were safe with her expertise. She knew how to handle business.

Isabella wasn't the only financial advisor choosing to habitually flaunt federal monetary regulations. She was just the most successful and uninhibited. She didn't consider her behavior as doing anything morally wrong. Everybody was cutting corners for simplicity's sake. Taking chances was just good business. Everything was wonderful. Isabella and her colleagues were habitually ignoring established business ethics rules and interpreting the law to suit their financial goals. Everyone was making a substantial amount of money. Everything was wonderful, until the stock market crashed.

Isabella and her clients lost all of their investments. Lawsuits were filed. Penalties were assessed. New monetary regulations and laws were passed. The new laws and regulations formally required the practice of virtue when investing client funds and enforced the foundational concepts of Aristotle's Ethics Rule.

STRATEGIES FOR SUCCESS:

As Isabella discovered, the rules apply to everyone, even if they are financially or professionally inconvenient. We practice virtue, not always just to be virtuous, but because the consequences of noncompliance are serious and often adversely life changing. Practice fiduciary responsibility, and avoid liability for circumstances beyond our control such as stock market fluctuations.

Aristotle's Ethics Rule stresses character development through practice, and a rational state of mind. Perfect for creating consensus, a good reputation, and a successful outcome. Often, in the real world, it seems expedient to "cut corners" and ignore ethical considerations. When this has the desired effect, more ethical corners are cut, and a pattern emerges. Soon, ethical ideals become blurred under the guise of expediency. Eventually, the pattern becomes more and more egregious, until finally the results have negative repercussions. By then, it is too late to avoid disclosure and penalties. Ethical practices are always the best policy.

ETHICAL DILEMMA ACTIVITY:

Present a hypothetical ethical dilemma to the group that is similar to a real-life issue being considered, and have small teams brainstorm a solution. Each team will then select a leader to present their solution to the group as a whole.

DISCUSSION IDEAS:

Discuss group response to the dilemma as well as various outcomes and solution suggestions. Make special note of those suggestions that overlap between the various teams. Is there more than one ethical solution? How should we decide on a group solution?

THREE

BAD FAITH

"The safest road to Hades is the gradual one — the gentle slope, soft underfoot, without sudden turnings, without milestones, without signposts." ~ C.S. Lewis

"Bad Faith" is a self-justification strategy. The French existential philosopher Jean-Paul Sartre argued that people are radically and totally free. However, the price for this freedom is anguish and anxiety because we are responsible for our choices and their consequences. He created the term "bad faith" (*mauvaise foi*) to describe the human tendency to resist or deny responsibility for these choices and their outcome.

Self-justification is used as a defense strategy to validate unreasonable, even immoral, behavior. For example, when one uses the excuse of something external to explain the compulsion to act. Think "the Twinkie defense."

"Twinkie defense" is a derisive label for an improbable legal defense. It is not a recognized legal defense in jurisprudence, but a catchall term coined by reporters during their coverage of the trial of defendant Dan White for the murders of San Francisco city supervisor Harvey Milk and mayor George Moscone. White's defense was that he suffered diminished capacity as a result of his depression. His change in diet from healthy food to Twinkies and other sugary food was said to be a symptom of depression. Contrary to common belief, White's attorneys did not argue that the Twinkies were the cause of White's actions, but that their consumption was symptomatic of his underlying depression. Instead of murder, White was convicted of voluntary manslaughter.

Sometimes the cause of our bad behavior is related to our cultural, social, economic or other outside pressures; but more often than not, we chose to do what we feel like doing and hope to get away with it.

EXAMPLE:

As its Chief Financial Officer, Jack had been employed by the Magnum Company for 20 years, and had gradually been promoted to his present position on the executive management team. He loved his job almost as much as he loved his substantial paycheck. He grew quite attached to the amount of income that enabled him to provide an expensive lifestyle for his family and himself.

Due to a series of unwise personal investment decisions, Jack was experiencing financial difficulties despite his considerable income. He was embarrassed to admit his financial predicament, but he desperately needed his monthly salary. The company was required to submit quarterly financial statements to the CFO for approval. Jack started to notice discrepancies. At first, the amounts were minimal and could reasonably have been the result of minor accounting errors.

Each quarter, the discrepancies increased and were cleverly hidden within the accounting figures. By the end of the year, Jack knew that the missing amount was substantial. He suspected deliberate corporate fraud. Because Jack regarded himself as a person of integrity and strict moral standards, he felt compelled to report the discrepancies along with his suspicions to the company CEO. The CEO promised to "look into the problem and get back to him."

Jack waited for the CEO to respond with an appropriate solution. The financial discrepancies continued to increase. The CEO refused to respond to his repeated inquiries, so Jack reported the discrepancies to the management team at their quarterly meeting. He was informed that it was merely an "accounting change due to corporate investment decisions" and that his concerns were "unfounded" because in their view "there was no problem."

When Jack insisted that proper accounting procedures were not followed, he was told that he needed to be more of a "team player." It was clear that his position as CFO was in jeopardy if he continued to question the financial reports. Jack was frightened. He was too old to start over with a different job. The economy was weak and he couldn't duplicate his generous salary at another company. He knew that he was fortunate to have such a well-paid and responsible position. Jack decided to be a "team player." He was aware that something definitely wasn't right, but he ignored the discrepancies and "signed off" on the financial reports. When the fraud was discovered during a routine IRS audit, Jack was held accountable.

STRATEGIES FOR SUCCESS:

Jack found himself in an uncomfortable, and unfortunately common, employment quandary. He didn't want to submit, but he felt pressured and compelled to act uncharacteristically unethical. He ultimately acted in Bad Faith, and suffered the consequences because of personal justification, even though he knew it was wrong. Think for yourself and insist that others think for themselves and are held personally accountable for their actions. Carefully consider the repercussions both personally and professionally. What will happen if we act like Jack?

VISION STATEMENT ACTIVITY:

A Vision Statement encapsulates future hopes and goals. Bad Faith is inherently unacceptable in an optimistic vision of the future. Working in small teams, have the participants create a Vision Statement for the group. Post each team's statement so that participants can read the similarities and differences. Cooperate to create a group Vision Statement incorporating the team ideas.

DISCUSSION IDEAS:

Will the vision change as the group progresses? How often should the group revisit the Vision Statement?

FOUR

BEHAVIORISM

"Laws too gentle are seldom obeyed; too severe, seldom executed."
~ Benjamin Franklin

Behaviorism is a psychological theory introduced by John B. Watson in the early 20th century. Watson sought to examine human behavior using observational methods to study human choice by eliminating any consideration of human thoughts, feelings or desires. Nearly a century after Behaviorism was first proposed, psychologist B.F. Skinner developed his theories of "radical behaviorism" and "operant conditioning." These concepts form the basis of contemporary learning theory.

Dr. Skinner developed ideas of reward and withdrawal of reward (often misunderstood as "cruelty" or "punishment") as motivators for human activity. He also envisioned a utopian society where all citizens were properly conditioned to behave in a socially acceptable and predictable manner.

The desirability and practicality of a carefully engineered utopian society is a hotly debated idea. However, as a practical application, Skinner also determined that rewards (added or subtracted) are substantially more effective than using punishment to influence human behavior.

EXAMPLE:

Ella had worked at the same mid-level management job with the same company for more than 25 years. She was a non-managerial employee in the Human Resources department. Her official title was "Internal Human Resources Director," which meant that she resolved petty disputes between disgruntled employees. She sat in her cubicle day-after-day reviewing workplace complaints and settling minor disputes. Bored with her job, and easily annoyed by the employees who solicited her assistance, Ella put in the hours at the office, but no longer put in much effort.

The company was acquired in a merger deal. All of the employees, even those with more than 25 years of experience, were required to submit to an employment review. In addition, an outside efficiency expert was hired to assess each employee, their job description, and their usefulness to the company. The efficiency expert determined that there were too many Internal Human Resources Directors. Someone would be fired.

When faced with potential unemployment, Ella was no longer bored or annoyed. She put a great deal of time and effort into successfully resolving employee disputes. Complaints were effectively resolved, and disputes were successfully negotiated. The employees were satisfied and impressed. Ella became the highest rated Internal Human Resources Director on employee satisfaction surveys.

The new management instituted a reward system based upon satisfaction survey results. Because of her exemplary performance, Ella was awarded the honor of "Employee of the Year." The reward included an engraved plaque to display in her office and her photo prominently displayed in the corporate lobby.

Ella was beyond proud. Whenever she walked through the lobby, someone recognized her and commented on her achievement. Her co-workers were constantly striving for excellence and aspired to be the next "Employee of the Year." All of a sudden, this company became a great place to work.

How did operant conditioning make a difference here? Would Skinner say this was a radical behaviorists example of rewards-based change? If yes, how might others import these findings in their own setting? The new work environment created reward-based employee competition that was highly productive for the employer, and highly motivating for the employees.

STRATEGIES FOR SUCCESS:

The reward needs to be something worth striving to attain. Ella was delighted to be recognized as the "Employee of the Year," but her reward was retention of her employment and assurance of future success if she continued to perform above average. Recognition, prizes, financial incentives, and other tokens of appreciation are all Behaviorism tools. It seems childish, but receiving a reward or imagining NOT receiving one when others do, no matter how small, can be a successful motivator.

FAVORITE REWARD ACTIVITY:

Give each participant two index cards on which to anonymously write their favorite rewards for successfully executing a goal and explain "why." Collect the cards, read them out loud to the group, and categorize them with group participation.

DISCUSSION IDEAS:

Discuss the similarities and differences in what people value as a reward. Were most of the rewards monetary? What type of recognition was most desired?

FIVE

THE BUTTERFLY EFFECT

*"Each smallest act of kindness reverberates across great distances and spans of time –
affecting lives unknown to the one who's generous spirit was the source
of this good echo. Because kindness is passed on and grows each time it's passed
until a simple courtesy becomes an act of selfless courage, years later, and far away.
Likewise, each small meanness, each expression of hatred, each act of evil."*
– Dean Koontz, From the Corner of His Eye

We've all had situations where a series of small problems escalate into larger problems that, if ignored, quickly become disasters. Mathematicians refer to this as a "non-linear phenomenon." Small issues can have cumulative large effects. Weather forecasters call this the "Butterfly Effect." Theoretically, the movement of a butterfly's wings somewhere on the planet is sufficient to change the weather.

Even though the "Butterfly Effect" is more sci-fi fable than proven scientific fact — first mentioned in Ray Bradbury's *The Sound of Thunder* — it is a real life everyday occurrence that small, seemingly insignificant, personality clashes can often fester and escalate very quickly into arguments. Sensitive negotiations can end in failure because of belligerent refusals to cooperate caused by petty personal disagreements. Like the movement of a butterfly's wings, participant sensitivities greatly impact negotiated outcomes.

EXAMPLE:

William was having a bad day. Nothing particularly momentous had happened. There had been a steady stream of small annoyances from the moment he had woken-up. He had no hot water for his morning shower. His wife was sick and couldn't take the kids to school. William was late to work because of traffic, and the school drop-off detour, and therefore missed the mandatory Monday morning meeting where weekly assignments were scheduled. William was assigned the less desirable "leftovers" for the entire week.

One of the management team members called to report that he was sick, and William would have to "cover" at a meeting that had been scheduled in two hours. He was unprepared and the client was unsympathetic. William was in a foul mood; nothing was going right.

William yelled at administrative support staff, accusing them of "incompetence." He argued with clients. He felt unreasonable, stressed, and frustrated. Clients and staff were shocked. William was usually polite, efficient, and reasonable in his business dealings.

William noticed their reactions, and grudgingly realized that he had fallen victim to the "Butterfly Effect" metaphor. He had allowed a series of petty frustrations and annoyances to build-up into explosive behavior. William regained his composure. He apologized both to the staff and the clients. He explained that he was having a "bad day" and promised that it wouldn't happen in the future.

STRATEGIES FOR SUCCESS:

We all have days when outside annoyances make us inappropriately unreasonable to the people around us. Our temporary unreasonableness can affect people that in no way created or influenced our unpleasant mood. William recognized the need to take control of the situation. The Butterfly Effect sneaks-up on all of us: The goal is to avoid and prevent escalation of petty griping, veiled insults, and other types of uncooperative and distracting behavior.

SEPARATION ACTIVITY:

Similar to the Butterfly Effect, the idea behind "six degrees of separation" is that by compiling our various unrelated personal contacts we would know someone who knows someone who knows someone famous. The small steps would culminate into a celebrity introduction. Task the group with determining how many intermediary introductions it would take to reach an influential person of their choice.

DISCUSSION IDEAS:

As an ongoing group activity, the participants could actually attempt to communicate with the chosen candidate. Did we get a response? Should we select an alternate candidate?

SIX

BYSTANDER EFFECT

"Small is the number of people who see with their eyes and think with their minds."
~ Albert Einstein

In an infamous criminal case, 38 witnesses watched a murder in progress. They all knew that the victim was in dire need of assistance. They also knew that other people were witnessing the same incident. Not one of them intervened or called for help.

Witnesses often refuse to react or even voice a concern during the actual incident, even if it is an inappropriate workplace situation that requires no physical intervention. When they come forward at a later date, witnesses explain that they wanted to avoid confrontation. They didn't want to "get involved." This type of non-intervention was termed "the bystander effect" by psychologists John Darley and Bibb Latane. Their ongoing research determined that the presence of other people reduces the individual sense of responsibility. We all think that someone else will call for help, intervene, or remedy the situation.

EXAMPLE:

Emily didn't mind being on committees, provided that they weren't too much work. She would faithfully attend meetings, if there was nothing more important on her calendar.

Other committee members enthusiastically volunteered for special projects. Emily did not. Workplace "teams" were committees with members from each department. Team membership was mandatory. Employees were permitted to choose their team. Emily chose the largest team available, reasoning that it was easier to hide in numbers. She also knew the team leader. He was, in her opinion, a "workaholic."

Emily was correct, the Team Leader was unable to effectively delegate. Team members were not required to actively participate; in fact they were discouraged from participation. The Team Leader would not only do all of the work, he demanded to take full control of and responsibility for all team projects. Emily was delighted.

The committee could not measure up to his impossible standards, so team members quickly learned to not try. When the Team Leader went on vacation for three weeks, nothing got done. There's a reason for the old truism: "When the cat's away, the mice do play."

After the committee had officially completed their assignments, the other team members complained about being "intimidated" into non-participation. They had witnessed the lack of participation when the committee was in session, but none of them had intervened, complained, or risked confrontation with the Team Leader. They had all hoped that someone else would take the initiative and object.

The corporate management team listened to the employees who complained. New team participation guidelines were created. Everyone was required to participate. Everyone was required to complete designated team assignments. Progress reports, submitted quarterly to the management team, were now required. The days of "someone else will do it" were over. Emily was disappointed because she could no longer be a passive bystander, she would have to become an active participant.

STRATEGIES FOR SUCCESS:

The lack of timely reaction to undesirable circumstances doesn't happen in a vacuum. All of the bystanders are complacent, and hope that they will not be required to step forward. Emily didn't want to assume extra duties, or potentially incur the wrath of her supervisor, but she and her teammates wanted to complain later about the lack of participation and progress. How much more efficient would it have been to confront the problem, and find a mutually satisfactory solution?

The "bystander effect" happens in every size group and in every situation. Everybody hopes that someone else will do it so "it" doesn't get done. The practical solution to prevent micro-management and ineffective group dynamics from preventing participation is to specifically delegate responsibility and task assignments. Accountability, and a procedure for intervention without requiring direct personal confrontation, is essential.

ELIMINATING BYSTANDERS ACTIVITY:

Bystanders distance themselves from participation in the group, refusing to acknowledge their team and community membership. Select one half of the participants and secretly assign them the task of specifically defining the word "community" within the context of group membership. The remaining participants will be told to define the word "team" within the same context. Compare the results.

DISCUSSION IDEAS:

Were there more similarities than differences in the definitions? Are the differences pronounced? Engage the entire group in refining the definitions of "community" and "team."

SEVEN

CATEGORICAL IMPERATIVE

"There are those who would misteach us that to stick in a rut is consistency — and a virtue; and that to climb out of the rut is inconsistency — and a vice." ~ Mark Twain

Immanuel Kant's 1785 essay entitled *Groundwork for the Metaphysics of Morals* introduced the moral theory he called "the Categorical Imperative." This term may be defined as a way of evaluating motivations for action. The theory generally postulates that morality should be consistent and generalizable. Therefore, everyone in a similar situation should be treated in an equal manner.

As an example, Kant gave us his own categorical imperative or ethical mandate by declaring: "Act only according to that maxim by which you can, at the same time, wish that it should become a universal law."

Most of us would say that Kant defined a universally useful moral code worthy of emulation. Kant's definition appears to be both simple and straightforward. As a practical matter, the Categorical Imperative is neither simple nor straightforward if one takes into account one's cultural context and social mandates. Morality is subject to interpretation.

Problems result when not everyone follows, or agrees upon, that which "should become a universal law." Outside influences such as culture, religion, and legal restraints influence the practical implementation of the categorical imperative. Personal opinions and preferences also influence real-world implementation.

EXAMPLE:

Joshua was a person of high moral standards. He understood morality. He had learned the proper, and only, way of doing things from his parents and teachers as a child. Joshua conscientiously followed their teachings as an adult. He understood that morality was tied to religious righteousness. Everyone he knew understood that religious righteousness defined the categorical imperative. It was obvious to him that his childhood lessons were correct, and beyond contemplation or discussion.

Joshua believed that only his religion was the "true" religion, and that only the "true" religion was worthy of being followed. To Joshua, people who insisted upon following other religions were considered deceived by evil forces. If they continued to follow the wrong path, they would be denied eternal rewards upon death. He always attempted to show these "Godless heathens" the proper path that would lead to Heaven. If they refused to accept his help, he would have no further contact with them.

Joshua followed the categorical imperative. He treated everyone in a similar situation equally. Those who were "saved" under the guidelines of shared religion were treated equally as brothers and sisters. Those who did not worship his religion were outside the moral code, and unworthy of equal consideration. They were treated equally as the demon "unsaved."

If outsiders converted to his religion, and became "saved," they automatically became "similar" and entitled to moral treatment. The heathens (those outside "their faith") could be taken advantage of both personally and financially. Joshua faithfully followed his own Categorical Imperative. He sincerely wished that his religious morality "should become a universal law."

STRATEGIES FOR SUCCESS:

We all have internalized moral standards that inform our personal categorical imperative. These standards are often an excellent moral guideline for dealing fairly and impartially with other people. Unfortunately, people like Joshua validate their own theory of righteousness as an excuse for bigotry. To test your own categorical imperative, ask yourself the following questions to reveal your mandates for personal and corporate ethics:

- What if everybody did what I would do in the exact same situation?
- What would be the result?
- Where do our moral values clash?
- Where do our moral values agree?
- How can we reach an accommodation and move forward?
- What else must be considered to work together ethically?

SAME BUT DIFFERENT ACTIVITY:

We can all hear the same instructions, and produce a different but not incorrect result. The trick is authentic listening. Hand participants a thick piece of paper and ask them to close their eyes and follow simple verbal folding instructions. No peeking to see what everyone else is doing! Everybody is certain that they listened righteously and have the perfect result, but no two folded papers are exactly alike although they are sufficiently similar to be recognizable as the same project.

DISCUSSION IDEAS:

Why aren't the results exactly the same? Was there a "right" and a "wrong" way of participation? Discuss accommodating diversity and moving forward in an ethical manner as a group.

EIGHT

COGNITIVE DISSONANCE

"The Human race is a monotonous affair. Most people spend the greatest part of their time working in order to live, and what little freedom remains so fills them with fear that they seek out any and every means to be rid of it." ~ Johann Wolfgang von Goethe

Cognitive Dissonance encompasses the old adage: "It is wrong to believe one thing, but do another." If you believe one idea, but then do something in contradiction to that belief, in the absence of any external justification for the change, the contradiction is resolved by altering the original belief. The "cognitive dissonance" is resolved.

In the Festinger/Carlsmith "boring task" study, students were paid either one dollar or twenty dollars to convince someone else that an extremely tedious task was actually fun and interesting. The task was the same for both groups, and the students were given the same script for "marketing" the task as both fun and interesting. But the results were an alteration of sincere belief to resolve cognitive dissonance.

In private interviews, the students paid twenty dollars admitted that the mandatory task was boring, but the students paid one dollar deemed the same task fun and interesting. Why? The students paid twenty dollars felt sufficiently compensated to lie for the monetary gain, but the students paid one dollar had insufficient external justification or profit incentive to lie, so they resolved their cognitive dissonance by changing their original belief. In the example case study, the incentive was monetary, but a desired successful outcome is also an excellent motivator. With the proper incentive, tedious but necessary tasks can be deemed interesting, and assigned tasks enthusiastically completed for the benefit of the team.

EXAMPLE:

Lachlan was a person of fastidious habits. He ignored transitory fashion trends, and regularly ordered tailored suits with coordinating ties and pocket-handkerchiefs. He always got a manicure with his weekly haircut. He enjoyed being meticulous and resisted getting messy, despising anything involving physical activity in labor or leisure. If said activity involved sweating, he'd avoid it like smallpox.

As Regional Chief Administrator of a multi-national charity working to alleviate hunger in under-developed nations, Lachlan placed workers in specific relief stations where people could receive hot meals and bags of food. He loved his job, and was very good at fundraising and organizing relief efforts. Oddly, Lachlan had never actually visited any of the impoverished areas that depended on receiving donations, but he certainly understood that starvation was an untenable situation in need of change.

The International Relief Oversight Committee of the charity decided to personally visit the relief stations in order to determine first hand their effectiveness and need for additional funding. All Regional Chief Administrators were required to participate. Lachlan was appalled. The trip preparation instruction letter listed required vaccinations and unpleasant medical precautions. The recommended clothing and supplies seemed careless and last minute. For Lachlan this was frightening, and not the least bit fastidious.

Lachlan begged not to go, but the trip was mandatory. He would either have to quit his job, or go on the godforsaken field excursion. He started to gather supplies, and grudgingly made a doctor's appointment for the necessary vaccinations. Lachlan had never been on an extended trip that didn't involve luxury accommodations. Having the need to purchase outdoor supplies ignited horror. Discombobulated, Lachlan consulted friends, relatives, colleagues and wilderness experts. They were all enthusiastic, and a little jealous, that he was going on an adventure.

Though still apprehensive, Lachlan started to feel rather pleased with himself; he was stretching his comfort level successfully, and it was exciting. He was forced to go, but he was starting to change his mind about the situation. The trip was messy. Hygiene was minimal, the clothing utilitarian and unbecoming, and the relief stations were in remote areas requiring hours of trekking. Though Lachlan was dirty and sweaty, he decided to enjoy the company of his fellow travelers. They shared an adventure, and discovered additional methods to prevent starvation. It was difficult, but it was also good.

When Lachlan finally returned to his office, he proudly displayed dozens of pictures from his trip. He was messy, sweaty, and smiling in every one of them. He still wore tailored suits, and he returned to his normal fussy habits, but he frequently talked about this first experiment as a grand "adventure." When the next field trip was scheduled, Lachlan was ready. His cognitive dissonance was resolved, and he was no longer appalled.

STRATEGIES FOR SUCCESS:

We all have preconceived notions of what we "like" and what we don't "like." It's challenging to change these comfortable ideas, and look at tasks in a different light. When Lachlan was forced to abandon his fastidious habits (temporarily), in order to accommodate the situation he altered his original belief to accept the specific situation and embrace it.

To comprehend how cognitive dissonance shows up in your situation, remember a past example or create a possible scenario. Consider external justification when a participant changes direction. If there is no external justification, cognitive dissonance may have altered the original belief. Recognize that this altered belief is now internalized, justified, and deemed the truth until proven otherwise. Just like Lachlan, we can "change our minds" and alter our pre-conceptions.

PRECONCEPTION BUSTER ACTIVITY:

Ask participants to bring an item (or image) that represents something they ultimately enjoyed doing although they were originally apprehensive. Ask each person to explain its significance and what it symbolically represents.

DISCUSSION IDEAS:

How did the participant overcome cognitive dissonance and turn a negative preconception into a positive experience? Was the cognitive dissonance permanently altered?

NINE

COGNITIVE THERAPY

"The measure of intelligence is the ability to change." ~ Albert Einstein

Cognitive Therapy (CT) is a type of psychotherapy developed by American psychiatrist Aaron T. Beck in the 1960s. His aim was to help his patients overcome difficulties by identifying and changing dysfunctional thinking, behavior, and emotional responses. He assisted them by identifying thought patterns and behavioral habits that create biases influencing how they perceive, act and think. This awareness could empower the patient to modify these self-defeating habits, and replace them with healthy alternatives.

Although Cognitive Therapy was Beck's treatment approach for mental illness, one doesn't need to be mentally ill to have internalized biases and fears. We all have habits, and preferred ways of "doing things." It's just "how we think." Problems develop when these personal biases, and often-unconscious fears, lead to behaviors that re-enforce the original (and usually inaccurate) assessment of a situation. As illustrated in the next example, an individual's refusal to participate in the discussion and negotiation process may be caused by cultural conditioning creating unrealistic assessments.

EXAMPLE:

Thomas was raised in a culture where women did not work outside the home. When women were forced into the workplace, they invariably held low paying menial jobs because they lacked formal education. He accepted that the educational and professional differences between men and women were just "the way things are." It was his duty to work outside the home, and a woman's duty to work inside the home. He thought the situation was a fact of life because he had not come to terms with his own ethnocentric and limited beliefs; he never had to before.

Thomas worked as an account executive in a multi-national corporation. His new manager, and direct supervisor Bella was a woman. She was smart, highly educated, professional, and extremely competent. Thomas feared and resented Bella, and thought her position was one that should be held by a man because men had families to support and protect. He refused to follow her direct, and very clearly stated requirements. He refused to participate fully in team directives. Surly and resistant to change his framework became toxic to the whole.

Thomas learned that in the multi-national corporate world, women are often authority figures with the power to influence those in lesser positions of employment. Thomas also learned that if he wanted to remain employed, he needed to revise his idea of "how we think." He was forced to learn a new, more cooperative, way of "doing things."

STRATEGIES FOR SUCCESS:

A successful leader will need to establish that the workplace requires everyone's full participation. It should be made clear that all opinions are welcomed and given careful consideration, but that bigotry and discrimination will not be tolerated. Not only is this solution a good business practice, it's the law and management acquiescence to violations may be actionable under Title VII. Privately and discreetly determine the cause of each person's reticence to change. Biases, resentments, fears and unconscious assumptions should be clearly defined, discussed, and collectively resolved or appropriately handled on an individual basis.

Thomas is not an egregious historical example. His original attitude is still prevalent. Stereotypes and discrimination have no place in the modern world, and regular professionally led mandatory cognitive therapy workshops where these issues are examined and dispelled in a safe environment are an excellent compliance tool.

POSITIVE HABIT ACTIVITY:

Habits that create positive group dynamics can be inculcated by scheduling regular evaluation sessions. Before the mid-session break, and again before leaving for the day, spend ten minutes as a group discussing what we have learned and accomplished.

DISCUSSION IDEAS:

What do we hope to learn and accomplish before the next evaluation session? What could we habitually be doing that would make the sessions more effective?

TEN

COMMON SENSE

"Everybody gets so much information all day long that they lose their commonsense."
~ Gertrude Stein

The philosopher G.E. Moore argued for "the commonsense view of the world" instead of requiring, as analytic philosophers often did, that obvious facts must be "proven."

Moore rather famously offered "proof" that external objects exist by holding out his hand and declaring: "Here is a hand" and then holding up his other hand and declaring "Here is another." His point was that commonsense truths, such as the existence of the external world, are universally understood and do not need elaborate philosophical "proof." In Lesson 40, we will also discuss Ockham's razor from William of Ockham. This metaphor refers to a principle of parsimony, economy, or succinctness used in logic and problem-solving. It states that among competing hypotheses, the hypothesis with the fewest assumptions should be selected. In other words, the simplest explanation is usually the correct one. The problem is that commonsense and simplicity are rarely deemed truly common or simple.

We can all agree that the external world exists. However, our "commonsense" widely held beliefs and interpretations of the world are often very different than the widely held "commonsense" beliefs and interpretations of other people.

EXAMPLE:

Chloe was anything but common, and she had very little sense. She was a prime example of the old adage: "Frequently wrong … never in doubt." She was a very competent and respected medical doctor, specializing in pediatric cancer. Her private medical practice was enormously successful. She was also the largest individual financial contributor to the local children's hospital charitable foundation. Her donations provided substantial, and desperately needed, funding for uncompensated medical care.

When she retired from active medical practice, because of her years of financial generosity, Chloe was appointed CEO of the charitable foundation. She continued her financial support by refusing to accept her salary, choosing to donate the funds back to the foundation.

Although Chloe was generous, dedicated and well intentioned, she was a terrible administrator. She was an internationally respected doctor, and had always been revered, her ideas were never questioned, her opinions were always accepted, and her instructions were always obeyed without question.

During the years when she was actively practicing medicine, Chloe didn't need commonsense, because she was treated like a Goddess. She didn't need management skills because her office staff dealt with the patients, and the media, on a daily basis. As is the practice of most surgeons, she appeared only when surgery was scheduled and let the staff deal with the rest.

CEO's need management skills. They also need to raise charitable funds. Chloe was antagonizing both staff, and donors, with her arrogance. She didn't ask, she demanded. Chloe loved the phrase "everybody knows..." and then followed it with a statement not congruent with that claim. Politics, religion, cultural references consistently revealed assumptions that were very far right-of-center.

The hospital foundation Board of Directors couldn't afford to antagonize Chloe. She was still a major donor, but she couldn't continue to be the CEO. They were losing outside funding, and she exhibited absolutely no commonsense as an administrator. They created an honorary position, equal in prestige to CEO, but with no daily administrative duties. Chloe loved it. She was pleased to be relieved of the day-to-day administration and annoying fundraising. Now she could enjoy her retirement and still maintain an active interest in the hospital foundation. Chloe was very impressed with the Board of Directors; finally they were exhibiting some "commonsense."

STRATEGIES FOR SUCCESS:

Chloe was kind-hearted and sincerely interested in the success of the organization. She was unknowingly causing administrative difficulties, and a formal "job review" would be regarded as an insult. Remember that the oft' used phrase: "Everybody knows _____" is never true. Everybody doesn't always know. Underlying assumptions need to be clearly defined and understood. Common sense is extremely uncommon; therefore we must learn to practice it. For example, the Board of Directors dealing with Chloe exhibited uncommon good sense by avoiding direct confrontation with an important donor and finding a solution agreeable to all parties.

DIVERSE COMMONSENSE ACTIVITY:

Show the commonsense diversity of what participants deem absolutely essential and obvious to them. Divide the group into teams of four to six participants. Each team will need access to a computer. Give them 30 minutes and a hypothetical $100,000 budget to furnish a two bedroom home using the Amazon website. The teams will report their decisions to the entire group.

DISCUSSION IDEAS:

Discuss the reasoning behind the different opinions. What were the similarities and differences? Was $100,000 enough money or too much? Did everyone feel that their choices were "obvious"?

ELEVEN

CONFIRMATION BIAS

"Nothing which is at all times and in every way agreeable to us can have objective reality. It is of the very nature of the real that it should have sharp corners and rough edges, that it should be resistant, should be itself. Dream-furniture is the only kind on which you never stub your toes or bang your knee." ~ C.S. Lewis

We all favor information that reinforces our already existing opinions and beliefs; it's human nature to want to be right. There is nothing wrong with seeking confirmation from independent sources that we are correct, the problem arises when we seek confirmation from non-independent or factually questionable sources, and deliberately ignore all contrary evidence.

Psychologist Geoffrey Munro calls this "the scientific impotence excuse." He found that when shown factual scientific evidence contrary to existing opinions and beliefs, research participants refused to carefully examine the evidence or modify their opinions.

In the "scientific impotence excuse" studies, instead of analyzing new and conflicting information, research participants concluded that the subject under consideration was simply not amenable to scientific inquiry.

EXAMPLE:

Riley knew that his opinions were correct. He was always correct. That's why his father had appointed him to be CEO of the family business. Anyone who disagreed with Riley was wrong. He simply didn't allow disagreement on his management committee. Riley considered irrelevant all information contradicting his opinions and beliefs.

The Carriage Accessories Company manufactured buggy whips. It was true that the market had declined in recent generations due to the decline in horse drawn carriages, but they were the last existing buggy whip company. Their product was exquisitely designed from the finest materials, and they still sold a substantial number of whips to collectors and enthusiasts.

The corporate Board of Directors, and the management committee, wanted to increase sales by globally advertising and selling the buggy whips using the Internet. Riley vehemently objected to the idea of Internet sales. He insisted that buggy whips were an old-fashioned handmade traditional luxury item, and they needed to be sold in an atmosphere of grace and sophistication. They should not be sold to purchasers sitting at home in their pajamas in front of a computer. Their buggy whips were too special to be sold and advertised in such a vulgar manner!

Riley used the Internet to research information, and access marketing research studies. He was only interested in information validating his opinions. Riley found information clearly indicating that people greatly enjoy shopping in physical stores because of the personal interaction. He also found studies "proving" that online purchasing was inappropriate for high-end traditional items, like buggy whips.

The management committee, and the Board of Directors, disagreed with his research. They used the Internet to research information, and access marketing research studies, validating their opinion that specialty retailing required an online presence. Their information clearly indicated that the person-to-person shopping experience, even in specialty shops, was no longer economically viable for high-end traditional items. Consumers enjoyed the convenience of shopping online. Research indicated that an online presence was the best way to create a global market for expensive specialty goods.

They decided to compromise. The buggy whips would still be marketed through specialty retailers in brick-and-mortar shops. The company would also invest in a professionally designed website to generate international sales.

The combination was a great success. The company became the leading Internet retailer in the buggy whip market. Because of their Internet success, retail store sales and brand recognition also increased.

STRATEGIES FOR SUCCESS:

Oftentimes we see what we want to see. Just like Riley's equine customers, we wear blinders enabling only the narrow viewpoint. Ask a series of questions: What are your strongest beliefs and opinions about your product? What are the strongest beliefs and opinions of the other participants on your team? Does the only evidence under consideration re-enforce these existing beliefs and opinions? Are you looking at all of the facts, and considering their reasonable implications? What is the source of the information?

INTERPRETATION ACTIVITY:

This is a keep-an-open-mind activity showing that facts and images can be interpreted differently. Show the group an artwork print large enough to discern the details and discuss the subject matter and the artist's viewpoint.

DISCUSSION IDEAS:

How do the participants "feel" about the picture? For example, I use art by the Surrealist painter Salvador Dali because he paints ordinary objects in extraordinary ways. What is the subject matter? How do the details tell a story? Is there group consensus or do we all have a different interpretation? Is this difference the "point" of artistic interpretation?

TWELVE

CONJECTURE AND REFUTATION

"The greatest general is he who makes the fewest mistakes."
~ Napoleon Bonaparte

The scientist and philosopher Karl Popper determined that scientific knowledge progresses through a process of "conjecture and refutation." To be valid, scientific hypothesis should be tested with the intent not to prove, but to disprove the theory being examined. Popper reasoned, "You can't prove a hypothesis true, or even have evidence that it is true by induction, but you can refute it if it is false." Popper's theory applies beyond the realm of scientific philosophy.

The billionaire George Soros publicly credits the method of conjecture and refutation for his successful investment decisions. Conjecture and refutation applies to all decision making. Opinions, ideas, and ultimately decisions should be tested to determine if the foundational premise is true, or false.

EXAMPLE:

Mia prided herself on being decisive. Her colleagues thought that she was impatient and impulsive, but she just refused to be hindered by too much discussion. Mia always chose to make decisions quickly, depending on her "gut instinct." She never reconsidered a decision and instead pushed forward. She ignored all factual research indications that her "gut" could be wrong.

Being decisive was her formula for success, and Mia was very successful. Her profitable stock market strategy decisions were legendary, leading to her position as Investment Manager of a major international Hedge Fund. The greater her success, the more confident she became. Mia started to invest in high-risk-high-yield investments that other hedge fund managers were afraid to handle. She wasn't afraid; she had her "gut" to guide her.

Mia knew that the investments were high-risk, and that there was a great chance of losing substantial fund money. She ignored the risks, and didn't bother to examine any of the investment financial records for discrepancies. Mia was only impressed by the possibility of substantial gain if the investment didn't fail. Mia deliberately ignored the market trends. She also chose to ignore the market experts with their boring charts and historical research. She completely ignored the sound fiscal management idea of "conjecture and refutation." Mia purchased an entire portfolio of high-risk investments. When the economy was surging, she was hailed as a "financial genius." Suddenly, Mia's convictions became valuable; interviews and lecture tours poured in. Clients begged to invest in her funds. When the economy was no longer surging, her investments failed and clients lost money. Mia was no longer a "financial genius."

STRATEGIES FOR SUCCESS:

Gut instinct is great for characters in scripted TV shows, but terrible as a business model. Mia had short-term success, and became encouraged by favorable publicity to increase her financial gamble without reasonable consideration of the consequences. If a hypothesis, an opinion, a belief, a theory, or a plan of action cannot be subjected to the test of "conjecture and refutation," then it needs re-consideration. Before implementation, argue the refutations to test validity.

SUCCESS STORY ACTIVITY:

Divide into teams if the group is too large then give each participant two minutes to relate a successfully planned and executed business or personal outcome.

DISCUSSION IDEAS:

What do these stories have in common? Was the outcome successful because the underlying actions met the "conjecture and refutation" test?

THIRTEEN

DEDUCTIVE INFERENCES

"Man is many things, but he is not rational."
~ Oscar Wilde, *The Picture of Dorian Gray*

Socrates is considered the father of philosophy in the western world and his student Plato was his scribe. Plato mentored Aristotle and all three of them explored the nature and measurement of truth, ethics and beauty. Aristotle wrote a body of work that was to guide his own son entitled *Nicomachean Ethics*. In it he postulates that for certain deductive inferences it is impossible for their premise to be true and their conclusions false. His reasoning forms the basis of contemporary Deductive Inference Theory (DIT). The validity of the inference does not depend on the subject matter, but on the form of the premises and conclusions. Aristotle referred to these inferences as "syllogisms." The classic syllogism example: "All men are mortals." "All mortals fear death." "All men fear death."

To study the concept of deductive inference, present-day philosophy students read *First Order Logic with Identity*. These contemporary First Order Logic theories evolved from the works of Gottlob Frege, which are a modification of Aristotle's basic ideas, using mathematical theories and proofs.

EXAMPLE:

Cooper was a Dispute Resolution Counselor. He was paid by the hour. The longer the dispute lasted, the more he got paid. Cooper loved his job. He personally enjoyed arguing, and he enjoyed watching other people argue. The more heated the argument, the more he enjoyed it.

He especially enjoyed circular arguments with no reasonable conclusion because everyone would insist that their "side" was correct. These arguments could continue indefinitely, and defy resolution. They were very profitable.

Cooper understood that suggesting a false premise, in a manner that seemed impartial, would stimulate arguments and lead to false conclusions. These false conclusions could then be suggested as additional false foundational premises. Under the guise of reasonable deductive inference, the false premises and conclusions would build upon each other, preventing compromise. There would be many billable hours for an astute Dispute Resolution Counselor. Cooper was very astute.

Cooper was also a master manipulator. His billable hours were astonishing, and his clients were always in need of more "help." When his employer decided to make a real-life demonstration video, Cooper was chosen as an outstanding example of counseling skills. He was selected as the most successful Dispute Resolution Counselor because of his income level, and his list of repeat clients. Cooper's company obtained client consent to allow counseling sessions to be video recorded over a three-month period. Cooper conducted the counseling sessions in his customary manner.

When an impartial review team watched the videos sequentially the viewers concluded that Cooper was manipulating the parties into further argument. His employer, when shown the videos, was forced to agree. Cooper was fired.

STRATEGIES FOR SUCCESS:

Cooper actually understood the concept of deductive inference theory, and used it to unscrupulous advantage. Deductive inference influences the core foundational premise for the majority of issues under discussion. Questions to consider: What is the foundational premise, as in our example, for the counseling sessions? What needs to be accomplished? Are the deductive inferences valid? How do we know?

FINDING FOUNDATION ACTIVITY:

Practice asking questions and eliciting details to determine the foundational premise and underlying deductive inference, i.e., for example… Divide the group into partners and assign a project to plan. The first partner suggests a proposal and the other responds starting with "Yes, but…" after each statement. The conversation goes up-and-back for two minutes. When the two minutes are up, the second partner makes the project proposal with the responses now starting with "Yes, and …"

First Example…

First proposer: "I want to start a clean water project."

Response: "Yes, but we will need funding."

Reply: "Yes, but we can ask for corporate sponsors."

Conversation proceeds up-and-back for two minutes

Second Example…

First Proposer: "I want to start a clean water project."

Response: "Yes, and we will need funding"

Reply: "Yes, and we can ask for corporate sponsors."

Conversation format proceeds for two minutes

DISCUSSION IDEAS:

As a group, discuss how the format of the process influences the tone and cooperative response. How can we elicit the most useful information and feedback?

FOURTEEN

DELUSIONAL THINKING

"For, after all, how do we know that two and two make four? Or that the force of gravity works? Or that the past is unchangeable? If both the past and the external world exist only in the mind, and if the mind itself is controllable — then what?"
~ George Orwell

Delusions are real and reasonable to the person who believes them. Neuroscience deals with aberrant salience and the differing levels of dopamine production that create delusional tendencies. A discussion of medical treatment protocols is very interesting, but not useful for our practical purposes here.

We are only concerned with the behavioral manifestations that influence our person-to-person interaction. Scientists assert that delusions are not just mistaken beliefs. They are an unreasonable, and insisted upon, perception of reality. But is this statement true? The perceptions of reality are definitely not unreasonable to the person insisting upon them.

EXAMPLE:

Vladimir was a psychic vampire. Psychic vampires do not hunt or kill humans either for food or for pleasure. They feed off psychic emissions. It's actually a rather involved and complicated ideology. For our purposes, all we need to know is that Vladimir was neither a threat to others or himself; therefore, no one needed to report him to the police.

Vladimir would argue that being a vampire is a "lifestyle choice" and not a delusion. There's often a very narrow distinction between the two designations. Vladimir was a vampire, his father was a vampire, and his entire family had been vampires for as long as anyone could remember. They had lived quietly in their ancestral home for generations.

A recently proposed zoning ordinance threatened the quiet peace and enjoyment of his ancestral home. Ordinarily, Vladimir did not associate with common humans, but something had to be done to stop the commercial re-zoning.

Vladimir came to the community meeting opposing the commercial zoning proposal wearing his usual beautiful Victorian Vampire attire. He looked splendid, even the humans noticed. The community meeting was disorganized; they were poorly funded, bad tempered, and ill-equipped to prevent shopping malls from destroying the green earth. Somebody needed to take charge before it was too late to stop the destruction of the neighborhood.

Vladimir volunteered to manage the campaign. He was diligent, organized and determined. He rallied the other members of the group into an effective team that worked together and created a campaign plan to prevent the re-zoning. When they needed funding, he raised the money. When they needed signatures, he organized the gathering. When they needed votes, he planned the campaign. The group was a complete success. The commercial re-zoning proposal was defeated.

Vladimir returned to the quiet peace and enjoyment of his ancestral home, and to ignoring common humans. His neighbors returned to the quiet peace and enjoyment of their residential neighborhood, and to ignoring psychic vampires.

STRATEGIES FOR SUCCESS:

We may not be vampires, but we all have self-images that differ, at least slightly, from the public perception of who we are. When dealing with others, if their self-delusion is irrelevant to the issues being discussed, ignore it and move forward to a successful outcome, i.e., "Keep your eye on the prize." If the delusion adversely affects the potential for success, first determine that it is indeed a delusion, and not your own biases creating an unreasonable or unsympathetic interpretation.

If a delusion definitely exists, accommodate it as much as possible, and reason within the person's parameters. Factual presentations disputing the delusion may be effective, although a very deep-seated and pervasive delusion may be resistant to reasoning. Understand that the delusion is reality for the individual, and achieve a successful negotiated outcome.

WHO ARE YOU ACTIVITY:

It can be fun and informative to meet everyone in the group and have them tell you about themselves. Even if you perceive that the presentation is delusional, it is who they think they are! At the beginning of the first meeting, ask each participant to stand up and tell the group who they are, what they do for a living, and something interesting about themselves. If appropriate, ask participants to bring a sufficient number of business cards to distribute as they are speaking.

DISCUSSION IDEAS:

Was this a fun activity and would we like to have a version of it at the start of tomorrow's session? We could talk about different topics such as: favorite vacation, hobbies, favorite movie, etc. because the more we know about each other, the greater our abilities to work together successfully.

FIFTEEN

EGO THEORY

"The pendulum of the mind oscillates between sense and nonsense, not between right and wrong." ~ C.G. Jung

Sigmund Freud developed the theory of the human psyche or "Ego." His ego hypothesis has two interconnected manifestations. The ego consists of the moral "Superego" which is in constant conflict with the immoral "Id." According to this model of the psyche, the id is the set of uncoordinated instinctual trends; the super-ego plays the critical and moralizing role; and the ego is the organized, realistic part that mediates between the desires of the id and the super-ego. Freud described the super-ego as the internal force within the psyche that can stop you from doing certain things that your id may want you to do.

A modern representation of Freud's theory is the familiar caricature of the man getting advice from an angel on one shoulder, and a devil on the other. Undoubtedly, Freud would have been appalled by this simplistic caricature. He would have argued that the manifestations are sub-conscious, not independently conscious decision makers. Sigmund Freud theorized that psychological problems related to the ego were manifestations of sexual desire and repression. Contemporary psychiatry in the west deals with ego issues beyond the confines of Freud's sexual hypothesis. The psychological conflict between moral good and personal desire influences our decisions and our behavior towards others. It also influences their response to us. Repression of the "unacceptable" thoughts becomes a defense mechanism.

EXAMPLE:

James knew that he was an extraordinary person. He had always been more intelligent, more charming, and more beautiful than anyone else. Even as a child, he couldn't remember a single occasion where he wasn't the best.

Because James was so extraordinary, he felt entitled to indulge his personal desires. He didn't care about other people's opinions or criticisms. Other people were simply wrong. They didn't understand his importance. James knew that he was always right. He understood that certain behavior was technically illegal but thought most rules and regulations were written by un-extraordinary, undesirable, boorish people who were jealous of extraordinary people like him.

Because he was extraordinarily clever, James fancied himself above laws regarding moral personal behavior. They were written by, and for, inferior people. James regarded himself as a modern-day Casanova. Both he and Casanova were great lovers and chroniclers of sexuality.

In his mind, no woman could resist him. If a woman tried to protest, he insisted and forced his attentions upon her with the assumption that this was what she truly desired. Just like Casanova, he kept a diary of his exploits. James was intending to publish an instruction book, using his exploits as good examples. He regularly blogged about his sexual prowess, and posted explicit videos on his website.

Several female co-workers met with the police to file abuse charges. They also filed sexual harassment complaints against James personally, and against their corporate employer.

Once again, James was not stopped. His hand-written diary, blog posts, and videos were entered into evidence against him. The court ordered psychiatric evaluation labeled him a "sexual predator" with an "ego-driven personality disorder." James was astonished. He couldn't remember anyone protesting at the time. How could they? They should all feel flattered and driven wild with desire for his prowess. They had the privilege of being pursued by the most extraordinary person in the world!

STRATEGIES FOR SUCCESS:

Have you ever heard the expression, "the truth is subject to interpretation"? Courtroom attorneys know that witness memories are notoriously unreliable, and multiple witnesses often have multiple accounts of the same "facts" because they viewed them differently. Is James lying when he insists that the women were delighted with his advances, or has his ego interpreted the facts in his favor?

New research indicates that Freud's "repression mechanism" does exist, and can cause unpleasant memories of the conflict between good and evil (especially when evil wins) to be submerged into the unconscious mind so deeply that they are lost. What does this mean? It's possible, although unlikely, that even though there is objective proof of an event, someone may not be lying when they claim not to remember it. It is more likely that the person remembers the actual event, but has subconsciously interpreted the situation in their favor.

MEMORABLE MOMENT ACTIVITY:

The memory is often selective. Ask the participants to remember and write down specific details about a recently shared group moment. For example: the time, name of the speaker, presentation topic, food, and color of the chairs at a corporate event that they all recently attended.

DISCUSSION IDEAS:

Does everyone have the same factual memory? Do we recall the details incorrectly? Why don't we all remember the same facts? As a fun group experience, view and discuss the classic movie *Rashomon* by Akira Kurosawa which depicts the same event told completely differently by a variety of witnesses.

SIXTEEN

ERINYES

"Never do anything against conscience, even if the State demands it."
~ Albert Einstein

The mythical Erinyes (also referred to as the Furies in Roman mythology) were divine creatures of unrelenting vengeance. In the Iliad, Erinyes are described as "those who beneath the earth punish whosoever has sworn a false oath." They exacted strict punishment, regardless of any mitigating circumstances. Punishment was equally harsh for accidental infractions and deliberate acts. All human actions and behavior had harsh, and inevitable, consequences. The Erinyes were the vengeful enforcement Goddesses of the netherworld.

Unfortunately, it is not uncommon to find people acting like Erinyes. They strictly interpret all laws, rules and regulations. Common sense, changing circumstances, economic realities, and the specific situation are not considered. In an effort to control the situation, they ardently search for the "exact letter of the law," and insist that others join them in their quest for the one and only "right way." Deviation from the human Erinyes' decisions is prohibited, regardless of the circumstances.

EXAMPLE:

Charlotte was the CEO of a family-run company. Because she was the family matriarch, she had lots of rules concerning family and business behavior.

Charlotte expected to be obeyed. The family, and the company employees, referred to her privately as "Madam Tyrant." The rules were not written down, or disseminated in advance, so no one could know "the rules" in advance because Charlotte created them according to the situation.

The governing rules were subject only to her interpretation, and she became hostile when questioned. Any deemed infractions were punished severely, usually by dismissal from employment or disinheritance from the family. Whenever Charlotte decided not to do something, it was "against the rules." She refused to modernize, citing "the rules," and the increased expense. She refused to negotiate with employees, citing "the rules," and their obligations to the company. She refused all family member suggestions, citing their lack of experience and judgment. She refused to pay suppliers, insisting that all accounts would be paid "next month" or when the financial situation improved.

Over time, their company faced bankruptcy. In desperation, the family members requested a written set of company rules. Charlotte refused, insisting that the rules were all dictated by "commonsense that everyone knows." Charlotte was the company majority shareholder as well as CEO. She refused to interpret "the rules" to accommodate the assistance of a professional management team. She was angry, and vindictive, at the mere suggestion that her behavior was unwise. She refused all offers and suggestions, regarding them as punishable rule infractions unworthy of discussion.

No one was surprised but Charlotte when the company went bankrupt. The bankruptcy administrator ignored Charlotte, and her rules. The administrator hired experts to re-organize the business. By using company assets, they could pay debts and modernize. Employee benefits were re-negotiated. Charlotte was no longer CEO, and her rules no longer mattered.

STRATEGIES FOR SUCCESS:

Management, and family matriarchs, often insist upon strict rule interpretation as a means of retaining control when their position is threatened. Charlotte was reacting unreasonably because she was losing her status. Instead of fighting and allowing the company to slide into bankruptcy, the family members needed to recognize that Charlotte had become an Erinyes out of fear.

Rules are subject to interpretation. We need to prevent having the process hijacked by compliance arguments that obstruct successful conclusion. Ask: "Is the interpretation reasonable and within the intent of the rules, regulations, or laws? Does strict interpretation move us forward, or slow the process into a semantics argument? Are there mitigating circumstances?"

ANONYMOUS ADVICE ACTIVITY:

When problems occur, sometimes people unconsciously become Erinyes because of stress and uncertainty in finding a solution. Distribute index cards and ask each participant to anonymously describe a problem or concern regarding the specific issues under group discussion.

DISCUSSION IDEAS:

Collect the cards, shuffle them thoroughly, and read them to the group for discussion and advice on practical solutions. Depending upon time constraints, the cards can be retained and several discussed at each meeting until all of them have been considered.

SEVENTEEN

EUBULIDE'S PARADOX

*"Men, in general, judge more from appearances than from reality.
All men have eyes, but few have the gift of perception."* ~ Machiavelli

When does the definition change between a mountain of sand and a pile of sand? The answer to Eubulide's paradox is that the definition is vague and therefore must be interpreted in relative terms. The mountain will still be a mountain when it contains just one grain of sand, if the grains were removed one-by-one.

Are the issues a mountain, or a pile of sand? Do they seem insurmountable, or capable of negotiation? Do we see a mountain, or individual steps toward resolution?

The answer is in how we approach the situation. The more complex and varied the mountain, the more necessary it becomes to separately define and resolve each issue in a step-by-step logical progression. Each issue becomes a grain of sand in Eubulide's Paradox.

EXAMPLE:

Olivia was Chief Regulatory Compliance Officer for an international pharmaceutical company. She was new to this particular job, but had a great deal of experience dealing with regulatory agencies. Compliance was complicated because every country created specific rules and standards for drug distribution. The same product could be designated prescription-only, over-the-counter, for a specific purpose, or banned completely, depending upon the marketplace. In addition to different requirements written in a variety of languages, the rules constantly changed depending upon government, and consumer, demands. These sudden demands often were the result of unscientific media attention due to a small number of allergic reactions or drug misuse.

The corporate products were also sensitive to unproven media allegations because sick people were often desperate and expected unrealistic results. Olivia was personally sympathetic to those wanting urgent change, but angry that products could suddenly be unreasonably banned without scientific or factual proof of wrongdoing.

Undaunted, Olivia brought in experts to set-up a computer monitoring system to track changes in distribution regulations. The new system also tracked proposed changes, so that the company could send representatives to influence legislation. She hired a team of legal experts with multiple language skills to translate and interpret all international drug rules and standards. These experts also proposed regulatory changes to the appropriate government officials.

Olivia also hired a multi-national public relations firm to handle adverse media. Whenever concerns erupted, they responded with favorable publicity and scientific evidence proving that the products were effective and safe for consumption.

Olivia created a step-by-step procedure for tracking, recommending, and monitoring compliance and did so in ways that were easy to understand, highly effective, and capable of duplication throughout the corporation. She also created a highly effective emergency procedure for handling future adverse publicity.

The company was no longer legally vulnerable to international non-compliance lawsuits, and potential financial penalties. The corporate products received excellent reviews, and publicity was handled in an efficient and effective manner. The mountain had been reduced to manageable grains of sand.

STRATEGIES FOR SUCCESS:

Olivia divided a pervasive ongoing problem into a series of logical steps leading to an easily replicated solution. Whatever the problem, divide the mountain of complex issues into smaller sub-issues that can be resolved in a logical and manageable progression. Elicit help in deciding the scope of the issues, and their order in the progression. Problem-solving success is an excellent group motivator. Create a workable timeline so that progress can be tracked and celebrated. Working-down the mountain, grain by grain, will create enthusiasm to follow all of the interrelated issues to their successful conclusion.

ADVICE ACTIVITY:

Asking for advice is difficult because it's hard to admit that we don't know something. Soliciting, and accepting, good advice is critical to success. Give each participant two minutes to tell about the best advice they ever received, who gave it to them, and why it was so important.

DISCUSSION IDEAS:

What type of advice was most common? Work together to create a statement of good advice that applies to the group.

EIGHTEEN

EXPERTS

"It is unwise to be too sure of one's own wisdom. It is healthy to be reminded that the strongest might weaken and the wisest might err."
~ Mahatma Gandhi

Who qualifies as an "expert?" Perhaps we can decide that a specific educational degree is an indication of expertise. Substantial practical experience in the specific field of knowledge is another excellent indication of ability.

Psychologist Anders Ericsson and author Malcolm Gladwell's *Outliers: The Story of Success* suggested the 10,000 hour rule: Any individual can be deemed an "expert" with at least 10,000 hours of "deliberate practice" over a period of more than 10 years. Do you agree with this guideline?

EXAMPLE:

Marvin was a self-proclaimed expert. He didn't specialize because he considered himself to be an expert in everything. There wasn't a single topic that he didn't understand. He believed that he had everything he needed to excel in any area. He thought so, his mother thought so, and all of his online Internet friends thought so, too.

The problem was, not all of his co-workers recognized his brilliance and expertise. They didn't appreciate his abilities. Marvin knew that he was an expert because he had deliberately practiced extensive Internet research on a wide variety of topics for more than 10,000 hours over a period of more than ten years. His co-workers, and his department supervisor, ungraciously thought that his constant expert pronouncements were obnoxious and intrusive.

According to Marvin, they didn't understand how privileged they were to receive his expert assistance. So he decided to ignore his unappreciative, low functioning, ignorant coworkers. He was going to provide his expertise to corporate management for the improvement of the entire corporate structure. In fact, due to his management expertise, Marvin would soon inhabit a corporate office, and no longer be a delivery clerk.

The fact that Marvin had no formal training was irrelevant. The fact that he had no practical experience in this particular field was irrelevant. The fact that nobody had asked for, nor shown an interest in his expert advice was also irrelevant to him because in his mind he was a multi-talented expert and wouldn't be hired if this were not the case.

Marvin sent each of the corporate management team members a photocopy of his 600-page, illegibly hand-written, report detailing recommendations for improvement. The document was completely ignored by his colleagues and supervisors. Marvin assumed that the lack of response was due to lack of delivery to the proper important people. He re-doubled his efforts and sent everyone in the corporate roster copies of his ideas. He hand-wrote a 20-page thesis entitled "What You Are Doing Wrong" with recommendations he discovered on the Internet.

Management noticed. They decided to consult an expert before responding to the recommendations Marvin suggested. Management hired a medical board certified psychiatrist with many years of expertise in personality disorders to read the recommendation thesis. She determined that Marvin posed no imminent danger but she did recommend they send Marvin a generic note of appreciation, and immediate dismissal from employment. He was deeply gratified by the corporate note of appreciation and figured he was "let go" because some people envied his genius and others wanted him to move up to the top rung. Flattered, he assumed they all fought for his allegiance and both lost.

STRATEGIES FOR SUCCESS:

Beware of self-proclaimed experts; "being wrong" is their usual area of expertise! A legitimate expert certainly needs no formal training, practical experience is often more important than a specialty college degree, but Marvin had no reasonable claim to expertise. Ask for professional, reputable, recent, and verifiable references to specifically validate the claimed expertise.

GROUP MASCOT ACTIVITY:

Have participants use their combined expertise to create a drawing depicting their ideas for a symbolic group mascot. Allow the group fifteen minutes to strategize and decide how their mascot should look.

DISCUSSION IDEAS:

What mascot physical characteristics are symbolic of the group? How should we decide? Designate a volunteer to be the artist who renders the drawing with expert advice from the group.

NINETEEN

FACIAL ACTION CODING SYSTEM (FACS)

"There is a difference between imitating a good man and counterfeiting him."
~ Benjamin Franklin

Charles Darwin theorized that human facial expressions were universal. In his travels to remote areas as an evolutionary scientist, he observed that emotional reactions registered as facial expressions in similar manners among dissimilar people.

Paul Ekman expanded upon the "universal facial expression" hypothesis by researching cross-cultural facial reactions to identical stimuli. He found that we indeed all share the same facial reactions to convey emotions such as surprise, fright, sadness, elation and anger. Ekman used this research to create the FACS a very detailed study from the perspective of negotiation tactics that categorizes and documents all facial expressions according to which muscles or "action units" are in use.

On a very practical level, if facial expression is the universal language of emotional reaction, we can gauge emotional response through close observation. Facial expression is an integral component of the observation of body language as a method of gauging participant response.

EXAMPLE:
Katia was the chief contract negotiator for an international mechanical equipment firm. She frequently negotiated complicated contracts with clients, suppliers, and sub-contractors. Many of the contracts were with Russian speaking company management teams and contractors. Though Katia's grandparents spoke Russian, she only spoke English. The negotiation process was complicated. It was very important to negotiate

a favorable financial agreement, as well as favorable terms, because competition in the mechanical equipment consumer market was fierce.

Katia was an experienced negotiator, but she was at a disadvantage in negotiations when an interpreter was necessary because the other participants didn't speak English. She observed that everyone spoke to the interpreter, or to their colleagues, in their common language, but not directly to each other. She decided to not concentrate only on the words. The third party interpreter might be inexact. Instead, she focused on the tone of voice and body language of the primary speaker.

Katia listened for evidence of excitement and for hesitation. She watched for behavior indicating nervousness, or confidence. She watched facial expressions, especially the eyes because she truly believed Shakespeare's idea that "the eyes are the windows to the soul." Katia watched and listened when the participants conferred among themselves.

She didn't understand their exact words, but had a strong sense for the emotion of the conversation. When she spoke, she was careful to control her voice and expression. She gained a worldwide reputation as a highly successful negotiator. Katia contended that all she did was "watch and listen."

STRATEGIES FOR SUCCESS:

There's an old poker-playing adage: "In poker, you never play the cards, you play your opponents." All negotiations are like poker games. Because Katia learned to carefully play the game, she was the jackpot winner. Observation is essential even if all parties are speaking the same language. Carefully observe facial reactions, body language, and vocal intonation. They will mirror participant thoughts, and indicate how to proceed.

EXPRESSION ACTIVITY:

Practice both reading and conveying emotions through facial expression. Divide the group evenly into audience members and actors. The actors receive a random card with an emotion written on it that they are to convey to the audience using only facial expression. After several emotions have been successfully conveyed, the participants switch roles and the new actors receive new emotions cards.

DISCUSSION IDEAS:

Why were there misinterpretations? How exaggerated were the facial expressions? Discuss the real-life use of subtle nuance.

TWENTY

FIVE PERSONALITY TRAITS

"I keep six honest serving-men they taught me all I know; their names are 'What' and 'Why' and 'When' and 'How' and 'Where' and 'Who'." ~ Rudyard Kipling

In Greco-Roman times there was a belief about human nature derived from one of "The Four Humors" known as: choleric, phlegmatic, sanguine, and melancholy. Later, the Greek physician Hippocrates (460-370 BCE) incorporated this idea by theorizing that all people have personality structures that fall within one of these four categories. Emulating the ancient Greek physicians, modern psychology names five personality traits: extraversion, agreeableness, openness, neuroticism, and conscientiousness. Technology has advanced, terms have become more sophisticated and nuanced but, fundamentally, people haven't changed much since the ancient Greeks.

These five general personality traits can be valuable guides when dealing with personality conflicts. They allow us to assess participant personality types early in the negotiation process. We can then vary our approach accordingly. Of course, people have complex personalities. There is no definite "line" separating types, and the distinctions become blurred.

There is also some contemporary disagreement within the fields (too many to ever be generalizable) of psychology concerning the designation of five general traits. In the mid 1950s, the father of cognitive clinical psychology George A. Kelly had a theory of personality based on what he called, Personal Construct Psychology. These "constructs" are a way of interpreting and anticipating other people's reactions by using internalized ideas of reality in order to understand the external world. The idea that we construe reality is also applied in the business context to decision-making and interpretation of other people's worldviews. Kelly claims, "Every man is, in his own particular way, a scientist.... We build theories — often stereotypes — about other people and also try to control them or impose on others our own theories so that we are better able to predict their actions." This type of in-depth assessment of the individual is a valuable negotiation tool.

EXAMPLE:

Sienna had a complex personality. She didn't fit neatly into any of the five general psychological personality traits because she didn't fit into just one trait. In different degrees, Sienna crossed over into all five of them. Within a 24-hour period she could be extraverted, agreeable, open, and neurotic, depending upon the immediate circumstances. She did have one dominant personality trait: Sienna loved Sienna.

She was extraverted and agreeable when something was being done for her benefit. Sienna was charming when it suited her, and unpleasantly neurotic when she was no longer interested. Sienna was extremely open to new ideas, especially the ones that benefitted her personally or financially. She was conscientious and careful concerning money. If the situation was not to her benefit, Sienna threw a verbal tantrum until circumstances changed in her favor. When the situation worked for her, she'd be sure to maintain the status quo. Sienna was a human being and like all human beings, including our clients, colleagues and family members, she had complex needs, and adapted her response according to the immediate circumstances.

STRATEGIES FOR SUCCESS:

Because we are all human, our personality traits are flexible and influence behavior depending upon the situation. Sienna shows us that the list of five psychological designations is a general reference point, not an exclusionary list of definite attributes. The five factors are continuous dimensions (like strength) and everyone has aspects of all five in their personality. Everyone also exhibits a foundational "core" type evidenced by their behavior. Whether you use the "five traits" or the "personal construct" theory, look for the "core" personality indicators in others and, most importantly, in your own behavior.

DEFINE ME ACTIVITY:

Dominant personality types can be evidenced by the manner in which participants choose to define themselves. Distribute index cards and give participants five minutes to write down interesting facts about themselves that correspond to the letters in either their first or last name. Allow use of a nickname or abbreviation if the names are very long. Take turns sharing the results.

DISCUSSION IDEAS:

Was it difficult to define ourselves? What were the most common characteristics? Were all of the traits positive?

TWENTY ONE

FUNDAMENTAL ATTRIBUTION ERROR

"We are chameleons, and our partialities and prejudices change places with an easy and blessed facility." ~ Mark Twain

Attribution is the psychological process that we employ to determine causation. Of course, in our opinion, negative causation is never actually caused by us! Psychologist Lee Ross coined the phrase "Fundamental Attribution Error." Dr. Ross found that we tend to attribute our own less-than-stellar behavior to outside causes, but we attribute the same behavior in others to their personality flaws.

Fundamental Attribution Error is a form of cognitive bias. We understand our own compelling circumstances and internal feelings, but we don't understand the compelling circumstances and internal feelings of others. Instead of being generous and understanding, humans tend to judge other humans on the basis of their overt behavior, seen through the lens of personal cognitive bias.

EXAMPLE:

Ethan was new to the neighborhood and thrilled to be living in his first single-family home in the suburbs of Los Angeles. He didn't understand what his new neighbors expected as he had always lived in a rental apartment in a large multi-unit complex. As a social courtesy, whenever another renter was in the building elevator, Ethan avoided eye contact. If he noticed someone else in a public area, he never intruded into their "personal space."

Ethan understood, and appreciated, the unwritten privacy rules of living in an urban environment. He had never before encountered the suburban unwritten rules of social connection. He was shocked by the overt social behavior of his new neighbors. What type of people acted in such an invasive manner? The neighbors were not only making eye contact, they were acting as though they were lifelong friends with Ethan. Whenever he ventured outside his door, someone invariably waved and ran towards him, violating his personal space. Ethan felt forced to sneak into his own home to avoid confrontation.

When Ethan came home from work one Friday evening, he found two of his new neighbors standing on his doorstep with a basket of jams and jellies. His first reaction was, "Are they trying to sell me something?" Frustrated and baffled he knew he'd need to remind them to make an appointment if they ever wanted anything from him.

To make matters worse, it was obvious that the neighbors expected him to welcome them inside his home for coffee and chitchat. Ethan was appalled. He wasn't exactly unfriendly, but he did like his privacy. He didn't know these people who were presumptuously inviting themselves into his home. Ethan dashed into his house, and slammed the door.

STRATEGIES FOR SUCCESS:

Ethan misunderstood his neighbors, and they misunderstood him. Everyone was attempting to act in a welcoming and civil manner, but they were frustrated by cultural dissonance. How often have we interpreted the actions of others unfavorably due to our personal experiences and pre-conceptions? Consciously think about your cognitive bias, and the cognitive bias of the other participants, before coming to conclusions. Have we made a fundamental attribution error that prevents us from considering alternative options and potential outcomes?

MISSION STATEMENT ACTIVITY:

Collaboratively create a Mission Statement to prevent misunderstandings involving the group purpose and goals. The Mission Statement should define what you intend to do, and how you intend to do it.

DISCUSSION IDEAS:

Were you surprised by the diversity of participant interpretation of the Mission? Will the Mission Statement need modification as we progress? How often should we re-assess the statement?

TWENTY TWO

GAME THEORY

"I was seldom able to see an opportunity until it had ceased to be one."
~ Mark Twain

If you want to win, you need to know how to play the game. "Game Theory" is applied mathematics seeking to answer the question: "What strategy should be adopted, given that we do not know what anyone else is thinking?" When Katia used the Facial Action Coding System (FACS) in Chapter 19, she was applying a strategy based upon physical observation. Game Theory takes the negotiation process one step further by adding strategies based upon psychological observation.

EXAMPLE:

Jessica loved playing poker. She played for amusement, and for extra cash. She played as a challenge to her friends, family, and colleagues. She loved playing poker because she was exceptionally good at it, and she usually won. Jessica understood that poker is more than "just a card game." In poker, you play your cards, but more importantly, you play your opponents. Experienced players watch for physical "tells," unconscious eye and facial movements, as well as signs of nervousness or indecision, that indicate whether or not a player is bluffing.

Bluffing is an integral part of the game. Jessica was an expert. She was also an experienced and successful negotiator. She analyzed negotiation opponents in the same manner as poker players. It wasn't exactly a gambling game of "chance," but opponents attempted to negotiate settlements by not "showing their hands," and they frequently tried bluffing as a negotiation tactic.

Jessica was not fooled. She understood that negotiation and poker have a lot in common. Being able to "read" the players properly was an essential skill. Sweating, twitching, shifting position, nervous habits, eye contact, the need for frequent breaks... Jessica analyzed them all. Jessica was a winner. Winners watch intently, listen carefully, and remain focused on a successful outcome.

STRATEGIES FOR SUCCESS:

Jessica uses physical observation, as well as verbal clues, to create a strategy for psychological advantage. Next time you're in a conversation with another, listen carefully, and watch for the "tells." Demeanor, facial expression, tone of voice, and choice of words are just a few indicators of innermost thoughts. These indicators are so strong that evolutionary biologists have used Game Theory to theorize why animals, and humans, choose to cooperate rather than fight.

BETTER GAME PLAYING ACTIVITY:

Choose a recent news story, or highly publicized celebrity trauma, and discuss how the situation should have been handled. Collectively watch a videotaped media interview involving at least one of the parties and discuss their demeanor and choice of words.

DISCUSSION IDEAS:

Did they hurt or help their position? What would you have done differently?

TWENTY THREE

GROUP THINK

"Insanity in individuals is rare — but in groups, parties, nations, and epochs, it is the rule."
~ Friedrich Nietzsche

In the Milgram Obedience to Authority[1] — a.k.a. "Peer Shock" — study that we discuss in Chapter 39 the percentage of participants willing to harm another research volunteer for the inability to remember answers, greatly increased when others in the room were willing to obey. The participants had become part of the controlling group, and they were influenced to "groupthink."

Though Stanley Milgram's study was published in the 1960 Yale academic journal of social psychology, its practices were deemed unethical. Still, literally hundreds of studies have shown that, instead of reflecting the average position of all participants, groups make more polarized decisions than individuals. Additionally, group decisions tend to accentuate any initial bias held by the group members.

Yale University psychologist Irving Janis coined the term "groupthink" to describe extreme group polarization. The three conditions leading to groupthink are: participants are known to each other and like-minded; a strong group leader; and the group is insular, not considering outside influences or opinions. Janis gave groupthink examples including

---

[1] Milgram conducted various studies and published articles during his lifetime, with the most notable being his controversial study on obedience to authority, conducted in the 1960s during his professorship at Yale. He was influenced by the events of the Holocaust, specifically the trial of Adolf Eichmann, in developing this experiment.

the "Bay of Pigs Invasion"[2] which precipitated the US embargo of Cuba, and the failure of the United States Commander and Chief to anticipate the attack on Pearl Harbor.

Groupthink is pervasive. Committees submit to groupthink when they become invested in their positions. Administrations groupthink when they refuse to acknowledge changing circumstances or global trends in the political and socioeconomic environment among and between nations. Businesses groupthink and fall behind. Big groups groupthink and implode.

EXAMPLE:

Daniel understood how important it was to be part of the management level "boys' club" at the Acme Firm. That's how you got the best business referrals and made the most money. Although they didn't necessarily like each other on a personal level, the "boys" had done business together for years. They consulted each other, trusted each other, and shared opinions. Daniel was the most charismatic, so he was usually the spokesperson, but the group always agreed. Negotiation with one "club" member was negotiation with them all. The group was a cohesive unit, and the individual members always deferred to the group opinions and decisions. They didn't want to be expelled from the group.

The Firm was considering promoting its first female member to the management team. She was more than qualified, and a better candidate than the male associate under consideration. The "boys' club" objected, arguing that she wouldn't "fit in." The qualified female candidate approached Daniel, and attempted to negotiate with the management team. They insisted that it "wasn't her time."

Groupthink, encouraged by the "boys' club," prevailed. The less qualified male associate was promoted. The female associate sued for discrimination, and was awarded a substantial sum. The next time a female associate was the best-qualified candidate, the "boys' club" was not consulted.

---

[2] The Bay of Pigs Invasion, known in Hispanic America as Bahia De Cochinos, was an unsuccessful military invasion of Cuba undertaken by the paramilitary group Brigade 2506 on 17 April 1961. A counter-revolutionary military trained and funded by the United States government's Central Intelligence Agency (CIA), Brigade 2506 fronted the armed wing of the Democratic Revolutionary Front (DRF) and intended to overthrow the revolutionary leftist government of Fidel Castro. Launched from Guatemala, the invading force was defeated within three days by the Cuban armed forces, under the direct command of Prime Minister Fidel Castro. The actual "Bay of Pigs" is an inlet off the southernmost border of Cuba.

STRATEGIES FOR SUCCESS:

Groups have biases when the members have been selected because they are of "like mind," and the biases are confirmed and reconfirmed by other members in a never-ending loop of the blind leading the blind. Daniel loves the exclusionary "boy's club" because it makes him feel important and accepted. The female associate in our example knew that it is illegal to workplace discriminate under Title VII anti-discrimination laws, teaching the firm an expensive corporate lesson. Recognize the problem — and force the group — to think. Guard against becoming insular. Welcome outside opinions and advice. Rotate group members to encourage new perspectives and illustrate democracy in leadership.

OFF COUNT ACTIVITY:

Pass around index cards and display a large jar filled with pennies. Ask each participant to individually write down their estimate of how many pennies are in the jar, and their approximate value. Open the estimate for group discussion.

DISCUSSION IDEAS:

How did the group choose a number? Did it match any of the individual estimates?

TWENTY FOUR

HARPIES

"No one can make you feel inferior without your consent." ~ Eleanor Roosevelt

In ancient Greek mythology, both Homer and Hesiod (circa 750-650 BCE) use the word *Harpy* "that which snatches" to give life to the idea of vicious greed. They were personified in nature as the destructive force of the wind. The "hounds of Zeus," Harpies[3] were sent to torment and punish humans. Vicious, cruel, and frequently violent, they were sent to capture humans and torture them on their journey.

In contemporary meaning, the term "harpy" describes a greedy, malicious, predatory person. Although the term no longer literally describes a mythical monster, human Harpies have monstrous personalities reflected by their egregious voracious behavior. We have all encountered Harpies. They are frequently highly successful in business due to their aggressive and uncompromising natures, and highly unsuccessful in their personal lives due to the same character traits.

EXAMPLE:

Oliver wasn't a Harpy, he just liked getting what he felt entitled to, and he was entitled to the best of everything. It was obvious.

Not unlike Dickens's Scrooge, Oliver feared he was completely surrounded by greedy, lazy and predatory people. They were always trying to prevent him from succeeding. He had to constantly, and aggressively, protect himself to avoid being cheated. It took vigilance.

---

[3] Harpies as ugly winged bird-women, *e.g.* in Aeschylus' *The Eumenides* (line 50) are a late development, due to a confusion with the Sirens. Roman and Byzantine writers detailed their ugliness.

When Oliver's business partner died, the widow had attempted to claim a portion of the income producing assets so that she and the children could maintain their lifestyle. Oliver had amassed great material wealth and had profited substantially from his partner's death, but he didn't see why the family should have any of the money. They should get jobs.

Regarding himself as the victim, Oliver fought the family in court. He agreed to a moderate monthly pay-out only after months of bitter negotiation. Even though there was a court order dictating the payment schedule, Oliver delayed sending the mandatory payment every month. Every month, the widow had to contact his office to "remind" Oliver that payment was due. Oliver was always unsympathetic. Why should he make getting money easy?

The family fell behind in their mortgage payments. His partner's widow begged for more money. Oliver refused. When the house went into foreclosure, he purchased it for a cheap price. Why should he ignore a great real estate deal? Oliver was enjoying the game. He bragged about his exploitation of his partner's family to anyone who would listen. The widow sued Oliver, and his firm, under the provisions of her husband's partnership agreement. The case attracted media attention, which resulted in "bad press." Aghast, Oliver could not believe how the media unfairly portrayed the widow and children as victims, with him as the villain. Financial negotiation was a game for him, and it wasn't his fault that he was a better player.

Clients noticed the media attention, and started to ask personal questions. Oliver was extremely annoyed. He was excellent at business and made clients substantial amounts of money. Why should clients care about his personal financial dealings?

Oliver hated to "waste" money, but he was in the public relations business. He needed a good "image" to attract new clients. He negotiated a lump-sum settlement with the widow that was substantially less than she was entitled to, but she would no longer need to beg Oliver for payment every month. The widow accepted his settlement proposal. Oliver certainly didn't consider himself to be a Harpy. He was just a tough negotiator, and good with money. What was wrong with that?

STRATEGIES FOR SUCCESS:

Oliver felt righteously indignant when forced to settle because of media publicity. Legally, he was not required to compromise, and he was fulfilling his minimum financial obligation. Harpies are difficult because they refuse to negotiate or respond to requests until they are forced into a position where compromise is in their best interest. When confronted with a Harpy, the real-life strategy most of us use is avoidance.

If avoidance isn't an option, refuse to concede to unreasonable demands, and calmly assert your position. Mandatory arbitration, court judgments, and other legal recourses are fully and legally enforceable.

Although unfavorable media attention may produce favorable results depending upon the specific situation, Harpies generally enjoy personal attention and audience reaction to their malicious behavior.

Harpies, like Oliver, enjoy being difficult and pride themselves on their ability to drive a hard bargain. Righteous bragging is a favorite pastime. Refuse to lose your temper. Refuse to directly respond. Refuse to play the Harpy's "game."

EMPATHY ACTIVITY:

Explain that "empathy" is a valuable negotiation tool because it helps the listener to understand the other side. Discuss that "empathy" is not synonymous with "agreement." Have the group define the elements of "effective listening" and "empathy."

DISCUSSION IDEAS:

Was it surprising that "empathy" wasn't the same as "agreement"? Does agreement necessarily imply empathy? Why not? How can we gain experience through practicing empathy?

TWENTY FIVE

HEISENBERG UNCERTAINTY PRINCIPLE

"The art of being wise is knowing what to overlook." ~ William James

The Heisenberg Uncertainty Principle is a theory within quantum mechanics that claims we cannot know where an electron is located, and at the same time know how fast it is moving. We can measure either one or the other, but not both simultaneously. The harder you try to pin down an electron, the faster it spins around and attempts to escape. Just like imaginative ideas!

Committees, formal standards, and expert financial planning are excellent, and prudent, business concepts. Process is important. But sometimes, depending upon the situation, formal procedures are an impediment to success. Like the electrons in the Heisenberg Uncertainty Principle, the great ideas will attempt to escape. Experience tells us that it is possible to over-plan the process.

EXAMPLE:

Ava was the principal of the local Elementary School. It was a very good school, but it was part of the public school system. They seriously lacked money. The Parent Teacher Association (PTA) suggested producing a theatrical performance on the school grounds as a way to raise money. The potential funds were designated for badly needed student computers. The students could be the actors, and a small admission price would be charged. They could even ask local businesses for additional voluntary donations.

It wasn't against school rules. It wasn't against district regulations. Everyone agreed that it was an excellent idea.

An appropriate play was selected by majority vote. Parents, and teachers, volunteered to coach, direct, and build scenery. The students were proud and excited to be on stage. Corporations, especially those who employed some of the parents, offered donations. Ava acted as their liaison. She coordinated the volunteer efforts, and kept track of what was finished, and what still needed to be done.

There were no formal committee meetings, just phone calls and e-mails to keep track of progress. When something needed to be done, somebody volunteered. Enough money for twenty computers and "computer room" furnishings was collected. Everyone became excited about the next "annual" fundraising event!

STRATEGIES FOR SUCCESS:

Sometimes an idea is right and the group is in agreement. If it's a moral and legal course of action, there's no need for quantum analysis. We agree let's move forward. It's not rocket science, but we tend to overthink the process and insist on a formal management style. It is crucial to step back and realize that if the various participants are heading towards a successful outcome, allow the natural course of events to proceed unhindered.

IT JUST IS ACTIVITY:

Using the Internet comedy websites, compile and pass out a list of ten inoffensive one-liner jokes. Allow enough time for participants to read them, and check-off the ones they thought were funny.

DISCUSSION IDEAS:

Do we have agreement that some were funny? Do we really need to discuss "why" they are funny? Isn't it sufficient that we laughed?

TWENTY SIX

HERCULES

"Obstacles cannot crush me, every obstacle yields to stern resolve."
~ Leonardo da Vinci

The mythical hero Hercules was the son of a human mother and Zeus, the ruling God. Because of his divine parentage, Hercules was blessed with prodigious strength, great intelligence, heroic courage, and extreme sexual prowess. He was the hero who successfully wrestled with Cerberus — the many-headed guard dog of the Underworld. When Hercules died, he joined the Olympian Gods as an immortal. Hercules seemed perfect in every way. But he wasn't.

Hercules had an insanely vicious temper, causing him to kill his wife Megara, and their children. The ancient tales were essentially moral fables, and this egregious behavior could not go unpunished. The famous "twelve labors" (one of which was forcing the mythical Cerberus to the surface of the earth), were his punishment for committing these murders. Even Gods have their limits.

The moral to the story: "Nobody's perfect!"

EXAMPLE:

It's true that "nobody's perfect," but Ronin was less perfect than most people. He was very short-tempered and unreasonably nasty to his colleagues. He rejected even the slightest criticism ungraciously, and took offense easily. He was also the Board President's son.

Because of nepotism, Ronin was an executive member of the management team.

Ronin was also extremely opinionated. Unfortunately, his opinions were usually unreasonable due to personal bias, and unworkable from a business perspective. The other management team members were frightened of him. His father had company clout, he always sided with his son, and Ronin was easily angered. So they avoided him, and held secret meetings to discuss the "Ronin problem." The constant friction was impeding effective corporate process.

The management team decided to address the situation directly. They invited Ronin and his father to a special executive meeting. They openly discussed their concerns, and threatened to resign as a group if Ronin refused to behave in a more civil and professional manner.

Ronin flew into a rage, and attempted to physically attack the management team leader. Corporate Security Officers were called to restrain Ronin, the police were summoned, and a formal complaint was filed. The Board President was forced to admit that his son was behaving unreasonably. Ronin was officially admonished, and forced to publicly apologize.

He was also required to attend anger management training classes. Ronin did not change his personal opinions, but he did learn to modify his behavior and eliminate management team disruption.

STRATEGIES FOR SUCCESS:

Ronin, like Hercules, could get away with a certain amount of egregious behavior because his position was secured through birthright. Perfection is certainly not a human trait. People usually strive to adhere to reasonable standards of behavior, but everyone has a "tipping point" where tolerance erodes, especially when the workplace dynamic is adversely impacted.

Discuss the situation in an open, non-judgmental, and inclusive manner. Take a step back in the process if tempers are starting to flare, call a time-out, and re-focus the discussion before the situation becomes extreme.

CONFLICT RESOLUTION ACTIVITY:

Write the words "conflict" and "resolution" in big letters on separate sheets of paper. Post the two words at least three feet apart on a surface that can accommodate sticky-notes. Distribute a small packet of sticky-notes to each participant. Ask them to write a conflict resolution idea on each note and post them between the conflict resolution words. When completed, gather around the display as a group and discuss the posted ideas.

DISCUSSION IDEAS:

Why are the ideas similar? How do we define conflict? Can we create a conflict resolution protocol for the group?

TWENTY SEVEN

ICARUS

"You cannot teach a man anything, you can only help him to find it within himself."
~ Galileo

In the famous Greek legend, Icarus and his master craftsman father Daedelus escape imprisonment by flying away with feather and wax wings. Daedelus warned Icarus to avoid the heat of the sun because it would melt the wax and destroy the delicate wings of his creation.

Icarus, recklessly excited by being able to fly like a bird, ignored the warning and soared too close to the sun. His wings melted, and Icarus plunged to his death in the sea. The story is, of course, a morality tale warning against the consequences of rash behavior. Icarus was warned, and he fully understood the potential consequences, but he ignored rational conclusions in his certainty that he could handle flying too close to the sun.

We've all dealt with Icarus. Warnings go unheeded, reasoning falls on deaf ears, and exuberant (though reckless) actions create meltdowns. The group dynamic suffers, and the consequences are often far-reaching.

EXAMPLE:

Lily was absolutely certain that skateboards were the solution for global warming. Not fancy skateboards with motors, just plain pieces of wood with four wheels identical to the ones she remembered from her childhood. She knew that everyone everywhere, all across the globe, would switch to skateboards as their primary mode of transportation if the products were properly marketed.

She understood that the Internet was the way to reach millions of people worldwide, and she intended to sell the skateboards through her company Facebook page.

She also understood that the Internet was a powerful resource for global product research. Lily diligently researched the skateboard concept, and discovered that similar ideas using bicycles had been attempted, and failed. Reasoning that skateboards were not bicycles, she was undeterred.

Lily researched the scientific evidence concerning global warming. It was technically complicated, controversial, and frightening in all its implications. Lily was undeterred. Skateboards, with their non-existent carbon footprint, were definitely the solution. Undaunted, Lily was determined to save the world.

Lily was also the CEO of a prosperous skateboard company that sold sports celebrity endorsed, beautifully detailed, high quality skateboards to the skateboard gaming community. Lily had not built the company, she had inherited his position when her father died, and had never before taken any interest in product creation. The Corporate Board, which consisted of long-time employees with substantial managerial and marketing experience, was not pleased by her sudden interest in global warming.

Fortunately for the company, the Board was set-up as a democracy. Each member had an equal vote, including the CEO. The CEO received additional compensation because of her title, but she did not have veto power or any other additional influence. They voted not to create generic skateboards for worldwide distribution as a primary mode of transportation. It was a ridiculous idea.

Lily was undeterred. She created a charitable foundation to promote her idea, and solicited monetary contributions to donate skateboards free of charge to people in poor countries. Her foundation developed a low cost, no frills, high quality skateboard for charitable distribution. The donation skateboard wasn't a work of art, but it was very sturdy and functional. Lily's skateboard company produced it at a modest profit.

The company continued to be a success in the high-end specialty skateboard business. The charitable foundation was a success worldwide providing an alternate mode of transportation. They didn't actually solve global warming, but the skateboards contributed to the solution.

The company Board of Directors voted to become major corporate donors to the charitable foundation. They received international acclaim (and excellent marketing publicity) for their charitable contributions, and environmentally "green" policies.

STRATEGIES FOR SUCCESS:

Without imagination and enthusiasm the world would be a boring and uncreative place, and there would be no business innovation. The Icarus story reminds us that enthusiasm and practical application go hand-in-hand. Create a system of checks-and-balances that is rigorously enforced. Reckless actions should be identified and curtailed.

Icarus-employees/employers certainly need to be stopped before they carelessly dissolve chances for a product's success, but imaginative ideas are often the motivation for future growth. Remember that Icarus's father had a fantastic invention. Flying skillfully could free them from captivity. The wings failed because of reckless disregard for his father's warning: "You will drown in the sea if you fly too close to the sun." The wings failed because they required respect for "product safety," not because they were a bad idea.

CRAZY IDEA ACTIVITY:

Take turns answering the questions: What's the craziest idea you ever had? Did it work? Why or why not? If the participant doesn't wish to relate a personal crazy idea, they can discuss an idea that interests them, and its outcome.

DISCUSSION IDEAS:

How did we judge that the idea was "crazy"? Did it seem sensible at the time?

TWENTY EIGHT

ILLUSORY SUPERIORITY

"Everyone should be respected as an individual, but no one idolized." ~ Albert Einstein

We all believe ourselves to be "above average." Illusory Superiority behavior is more pronounced than Freud's ego-driven personality disorders. It's the certainty, re-enforced by circumstances, of absolute superiority over everyone else.

For example, in class-driven societies, individuals born into the upper classes feel empowered by illusory superiority. In reality, they experienced a fortunate accident of birth into a powerful family. This birthright, like any monarchy ("rule of one"), is interpreted by the individual and his minions as conclusive, God ordained, and evidence of superiority.

The superiority mind-set is not necessarily created by birthright. Power, money, and celebrity status all create the illusion. The arrogant behavior of even minor entertainment industry celebrities is a prime example. Problems occur when someone thinks that they are far superior to everyone else in the group. They are shocked when not everyone agrees with that assessment.

Like the Evil Queen in *Snow White*, they see themselves as superior examples of perfection. They feel entitled to impose their opinions and demands on the lesser members of the group. Obviously, everyone should want to emulate them, to follow perfection.

EXAMPLE:

Samuel was ordained "superior" by God and knew this without a doubt because he was the first-born son of a noble family. For sixteen generations, his ancestors had been superior to the common person. They were members of the nobility. He had inherited this superiority as a birthright.

Samuel was fond of recounting the intimate details of his family history. He found it fascinating that there had been many instances of family member inter-marriage over the generations. Superior and appropriate spouses were hard to find.

Perhaps because of this tendency to marry family members, Samuel was not very intelligent. He loathed anything requiring intellectual exertion. When forced to make a decision, Samuel liked to emulate whatever his ancestors had done in the past. He was also lazy, stubborn, and over-indulged. These were widely considered to be his finest character traits.

Because of his social standing, Samuel was head of the County Council. It was an ancient, hereditary, and purely honorary appointment, although he did have an equal right to one vote concerning council business. Samuel greatly enjoyed presiding over all of the Council meetings. He pompously insisted upon being formally addressed as "Your Lordship" at all times. He also insisted upon the promotion of ancient right-of-way laws over public lands. Samuel disdained the "peasantry," and wanted them to be punished for trespassing on what he regarded as his family owned rightful property.

Samuel contacted the media and issued a public pronouncement that the entire county was his ancestral property. He produced various ancient deeds and documents to bolster his claims. He also demanded "usage fees" from the peasants presently living on his land.

The other Council members, who were peasants, were not impressed. They voted (unanimously except for one vote) to amend the Council rules to include guidelines for fee assessment proposals, and for public pronouncements. They also took the right-of-way issues to the proper court, and received a ruling that the property was not ancestral property subject to ancient rights of nobility. Samuel was adjudicated to have no property rights to the county lands currently under private or government ownership.

Samuel quit the Council in a huff. Nobody missed him.

STRATEGIES FOR SUCCESS:

In our example, losing Samuel was a favorable outcome because his attitude was disruptive and his membership in the group was not essential to conducting business. If the disruptive member is essential, and cannot be removed, a more direct and hopefully diplomatic approach is warranted. Keep control of the process. Establish clear working guidelines, including time limits for public speaking, projected timelines for process completion, and committee pre-approval of all public media pronouncements purporting to represent the group.

EQUALIZER ACTIVITY:

Some participants are more experienced speakers, some have special expertise, and some have Illusory Superiority, but everyone is equal when trying a physical activity with their eyes closed. This is also excellent effective listening practice, a skill often lacking in those who deem themselves superior. Divide the group into partners. Give one partner a piece of thick paper, and the other partner a set of simple folding instructions. The participant with the piece of paper closes their eyes and follows the folding instructions read by the other participant. After five minutes, eyes are opened, and the results are compared with the entire group. New instructions and sheets of paper are distributed, and the partners reverse their roles. After another five minutes, results are again compared.

DISCUSSION IDEAS:

What do the results have in common? Differences? Would the results have been the same if everyone could look around while folding? Why were some partnerships more effective?

TWENTY NINE

INDUCTIVE INFERENCE

*"We should be careful to get out of an experience only the wisdom that is in it —
and stop there, lest we be like the cat that sits down on a hot stove lid. She will
never sit down on a hot stove lid again, and that is well, but also she will
never sit-down on a cold one anymore." ~ Mark Twain*

We can agree that the past influences the present. But is past experience always a reliable indicator of the future? Using past experience to predict future behavior is the realm of "inductive inference." Philosopher David Hume argued that "inductive inference" is not a reliable predictor of the future. He observed that it is logically possible for "all observed emeralds are green" to be a true statement, but "all emeralds are green" is logically false. Hume argued that although inductive inference often leads to truth, it is a circular argument to create an inductive inference rule, and challenged future philosophers to the task. Groups, especially committees, often become entrenched in circular arguments involving past experiences that prevent the process from going forward to a successful conclusion.

Contemporary philosophers have tried to create new rules to answer Hume's challenge. Max Black claimed to have developed an inductive inference justification rule with the statement: "infer that the future will be like the past." Does this seem non-circular?

Contemporary philosopher Nelson Goodman modified the rule of inductive inference, theorizing that the future will be like the past, but only in certain respects that are "projectable." This rule may be less circular, but it lacks defined certainty. How can we reasonably define, and evaluate, what is "projectable," and what isn't? As participants in a group work setting we are frequently asked to reasonably define and create projections for future growth. How do we do this? We consider past performance as an indicator of future performance while factoring in outside variables.

EXAMPLE:

Hadley, the CEO of his family's company, believed he knew exactly what to do in the present situation because it had always been done in exactly the same manner. The company had been family owned for six generations. Since the company's founding, every business decision had been carefully chronicled and preserved in leather bound journals. Hadley believed in strict inductive inference, i.e., he knew that contemporary business decisions should be based on these historical references, and the written list of business guidelines passed down through the generations.

The eldest son inherited the Board Chairman position, and followed the company guidelines created by their Founder generations ago. Hadley was the eldest son. The guidelines had always provided a "blueprint" for success, and Hadley saw no reason to change. He acknowledged that they were a bit patriarchal ("father rules"), the Founder had not even considered the idea of women professionals, and they were created in an era when the telephone was a new invention, but the guidelines ruled the company.

The other Board members viewed the guidelines as quaintly archaic. They were primarily useful when displayed, along with the leather bound journal archive, as a fascinating fact of anecdotal history during a marketing demonstration of corporate longevity, but the Board didn't agree that the guidelines should seriously rule the company in the modern world. They were discriminatory and unworkable in a contemporary setting.

The world of commerce was small and transportation difficult when the guidelines were written. Communication and distribution was now global, and in order to successfully compete in the 21st century marketplace, the company needed to expand into international markets.

Hadley balked. He didn't like new ideas or dealing with "foreigners." The Board insisted; it was time to take advantage of new technology and new market potential. If the company refused to recognize the present day realities, they would fail, and the company would become bankrupt. A compromise was negotiated. Hadley would be the "keeper" of the founding guidelines. They would be honored as moral and ethical corporate ideals, but not strictly interpreted to impede modern day business expansion. Hadley was satisfied that his family history was being respected. The Board was satisfied that the company could move forward.

STRATEGIES FOR SUCCESS:

Most anthropologists would agree that it is human nature to make "an inductive inference" that the past will predict the future, even though this claim is not logically reliable.

Hadley was comfortable using the founding guidelines as a "crutch" to prevent worrying about modern implications. Businesses with a long history of success become complacent and dependent upon following the protocols that have always been successful.

For generations, technological progress moved slowly, but we live in an era of great innovation and rapid change. Past performance should certainly be considered, but inductive inference cannot remain the primary guideline. Thus far, no one has created a non-circular argument that induction is reliable, but it is often true that past experiences are future predictors. What should we do? Learn from the past, and use it as a foundational idea for future results, even though every situation is unique. Inductive inference is a useful tool, not a road map.

ISSUES AND INFORMATION ACTIVITY:

Each participant receives two index cards and three minutes to write down the primary issue confronting the group on one card, and the most important type of information required to resolve the issue on the other card. Collect the cards, read the issues out loud, and group them according to similarity. Repeat the process for the information cards.

DISCUSSION IDEAS:

Is there general agreement in both areas? What differences were revealed? Do the information cards indicate reliance upon deductive inference?

THIRTY

INERTIA

"It's not that I'm so smart, it's just that I stay with problems longer."
~ Albert Einstein

When Isaac Newton observed and described the law of "inertia," he was measuring mass resistance to change in objects. Objects remain motionless until pushed. The famous formula is stated: "Objects that are in motion tend to remain in motion." Even though Isaac Newton was examining inert objects, the law of inertia can be philosophically applied to people, and their reactions to change.

Humans resist change. Even if the present situation is undesirable, we get used to the status quo. Change is frightening and uncertain. The status quo is comfortable in its sameness.

Humans tend to hold off on taking new action until pushed. But once provoked by pain, desire or necessity, we tend to remain in motion and become zealously goal oriented. For example, political revolutions are not usually caused by a single event, but by a series of smaller events culminating in the final "push." But once the revolution starts, it will gather momentum and remain in motion until the goal is either achieved or deliberately halted.

EXAMPLE:

As a recent college-graduate, Zoe felt lost during her first month on the job at the Biotech Company. She wasn't a "self-starter"; she instead enjoyed surfing the Internet and visiting fantasy websites. Her job requirements seemed to get in the way of her first order of business, entertaining herself. Unless the task was absolutely necessary, Zoe resisted giving it any of her precious "me" time.

While friends her age in other jobs tended to volunteer for work group related meetings and ask questions for help, Zoe only completed required tasks grudgingly. She did, however, like being paid.

Zoe attributed her lack of workplace motivation to her conviction that she was too smart to be under-paid, under-employed, and under-appreciated by her employer and besides, those menial tasks were meant for interns not herself. Her employer was under-impressed by her behavior and performance.

The company advertised a new position requiring technical skills, imaginative thinking, and timeline sensitive task completion. The job required a self-starter. The successful applicant needed to be creative, efficient, highly motivated and productive. Inertia and lack of enthusiasm would not be tolerated. The job needed enthusiasm and goal oriented motivation to keep "pushing" the creative boundaries.

Zoe wanted the job. She possessed the technical skills, but her under-performance had been noticed, and documented, by her supervisor. Because of her past workplace performance, her application for the new job was not being seriously considered. Zoe was suddenly motivated. She became an engaged team member with excellent, practical ideas and suggestions. She volunteered for corporate committees. She displayed advanced technical skills. Her workplace attitude changed from inertia to enthusiasm. She became creative, efficient, highly motivated and productive.

The Human Resources department, and her supervisor, noticed the change. Her application was accepted for review, and Zoe was hired.

STRATEGIES FOR SUCCESS:

Put ideas and plans into motion. Encourage individual enthusiasm and participation throughout the process. Move the process constantly forward, logically progressing from ideas and theories to pragmatic results. Zoe is an example not only of individual motivation, but also an example of corporate employee training and motivation. She was a poor employee until given the incentive of promotion to a higher position. Zoe understood what needed to be done; she just refused to act until properly motivated.

DANCE STEP ACTIVITY:

Group inertia sometimes occurs towards the end of a long session when everyone is ready for a break but time constraints require that the session continue. Instead of using the commonplace 60-second-stand-up-and-stretch, have the participants stand-up-and-dance! Divide the group into partners who stand three feet apart facing each other. Give the group three minutes to find similarities and differences with their partner. When they find a similarity they step closer, a difference farther apart. Change partners and dance again.

DISCUSSION IDEAS:

How many partners used obvious physical similarities and differences to dance? What was the next topic after the physical attributes were exhausted? Did everyone make an effort to discover similarities so that they could move closer? Was there enough physical space?

THIRTY ONE

INTROSPECTION

"The fool doth think he is wise, but the wise man knows himself to be a fool."
~ William Shakespeare, *As You Like It*

In his now classic text "The Principles of Psychology," William James wrote: "The word introspection needs hardly to be defined…it means, of course, looking into our own minds and reporting what we there discover." Introspection is the examination of conscious thoughts and actions as a psychological tool to determine the cause of ideas and behavior. On the other end of the self-examination spectrum, behaviorism (discussed in Chapter 4) modifies pure introspection by acknowledging that some mental processes cannot be consciously examined.

EXAMPLE:

Grace, a Health Director at Washington General Hospital, disliked introspection. She wasn't fond of self-examination. What was the point? She knew that she was perfect. Other people needed to think about themselves, especially the psychiatrist who suggested that Grace "reflect upon her attitude." In her mind, she didn't need to reflect upon anything, the psychiatrist was an idiot.

The psychiatrist visits were court mandated, but Grace knew what to do. She fired the psychiatrist, and found a new doctor with a better attitude. The new doctor didn't talk about introspection. He never used psychiatry labels. They just talked about Grace.

The psychiatrist wanted to explore what Grace was thinking, and how she felt about those thoughts. He made her think about her innermost feelings, and the reasons she was feeling them. They talked about her ideas, and how they influenced her behavior. They talked about her opinions. They examined her likes and dislikes. They made plans for her future goals, and discussed solutions for her present difficulties. They talked about her behavior, and its impact upon her success.

Grace and her new psychiatrist talked about her defeatist attitude, and how to change it. They made important strategic plans. Grace enjoyed talking about herself. She listened to the psychiatrist's advice. She felt enthusiastic and challenged to make changes.

Grace was delighted that she had changed psychiatrists. That introspection "stuff" was useless. She just needed to "think things through."

STRATEGIES FOR SUCCESS:

Introspection is important for everyone. Only we, as individuals, have direct access to our thoughts, pre-conceived notions, likes, dislikes, and personal opinions. Only we can decide the impact of our conscious thoughts. Introspection allows us to influence our behavioral responses, and our contributions to a successful outcome. If Freud was correct, our unconscious motivations (those convictions unknown to us) are made conscious through introspection with an analyst. Grace's psychiatrist helped Grace uncover and examine the hidden motives that might be thwarting her success; until they see the light of day, they tend to run the show.

The essential point to remember: Just as we make both conscious and unconscious decisions to work toward a successful outcome, or impede it … so does everyone else.

ALL ABOUT ME ACTIVITY:

Divide the group into partners. The first partner must speak for two minutes about themselves. The listening partner cannot speak or ask questions. However, if the speaker says something self-deprecating the listener must immediately say "objection" and the speaker must retract the remark and restate it in a positive manner. At the end of two minutes, the partners reverse roles. As a group, discuss the comfort level of each role.

DISCUSSION IDEAS:

Was it interesting? Challenging? How did you decide what to talk about? Was there a gender difference in the use of self-deprecation?

THIRTY TWO

LEAST RESISTANCE

*"The torment of precautions often exceeds the dangers to be avoided.
It is sometimes better to abandon one's self to destiny."* ~ Napoleon Bonaparte

The "Principle of Least Action" is a scientific term for the observation that in nature, reactions happen in the way that has the least resistance. For example, a straight line is the shortest route between two points; therefore light travels in a straight line. People also take the path of least resistance. We tend to be comfortable with the shortest path to resolution.

Although the issues are usually complex, participants are often satisfied with a simple explanation leading to a swift solution. They accept what appears to be reasonable, and refuse to engage in a closer examination indicating that their conclusions may be incorrect.

EXAMPLE:

Matthew always took the path of least resistance. He didn't like to work too hard. He didn't like to think too hard either. He was easily satisfied and didn't ask any questions. His workplace needed a computer system upgrade. Matthew was not in a managerial position. He was not on an executive committee, and he had no role in planning company expenditures.

Matthew was not consulted concerning the new computer system. None of the employees in his department were consulted. They were too "low-level" to have management input, but they did need to work with the system on a daily basis. The new system was a nightmare. Routine tasks became complicated. Matthew was forced to re-write a substantial amount of computer code just to make his software reasonably functional.

Because Matthew had trouble communicating how the new system worked, his co-workers were miserable. They wanted to know how Matthew managed to work the new system with such efficiency. Matthew did not like to admit that he had re-written his portion of the system. He was not paid as a computer programmer, and he was uncertain how management would react to his revisions and didn't want to make waves. He offered the simple explanation that his computer "just worked differently." His co-workers accepted his explanation as reasonable.

Management complained about the lack of functionality to the IT consultants. The most experienced programmer was sent to fix the problems, and he discovered the functional revisions. Matthew was forced to admit that he had tampered with the system. His co-workers and supervisors were angry. They had, without further questions, accepted the simple explanation with the least resistance. They knew that computer software was complicated, but they had made no further inquiry. They felt foolish because, if they had analyzed the situation beyond the explanation involving the least resistance, they would have realized that Matthew was using a different system. Further inquiry would have resulted in a more complete explanation and a tutorial in revising all of the computers.

The IT consultants were impressed, and offered Matthew a computer programmer position. Matthew loves his new job.

STRATEGIES FOR SUCCESS:

Although sometimes the simple solution is indeed the best solution, the principle of least resistance requires that we examine all of the relevant factors. As we will discover in Chapter 40 — using Ockham's Razor theory: *the simple explanation may indeed be correct* — there is no need to make the process more difficult than it needs to be. However, just like Matthew's colleagues who were frustrated by their lack of inquiry, we need to analyze the situation. Whether we're talking computer software or auto part packaging, has the solution been accepted because it's easy, and we can all declare victory, or because it's the best? Are we ignoring the complexity of the issues in favor of swift resolution? Should we analyze the situation more carefully, so that we don't feel foolish in the future?

TOO EASY ACTIVITY:

Give each participant three minutes to relate an experience where the solution of least resistance (the simple and easy solution) was either correct or incorrect.

DISCUSSION IDEAS:

How are the stories similar? Why did the simple solution appear to solve the problem? Was it a temporary "fix"? How did you discover that it wasn't working?

THIRTY THREE

LIAR PARADOX

"I have too much respect for the truth to drag it out on every trifling occasion."
~ Mark Twain

In the sixth century, Cretan philosopher Epimenides famously announced that: "All Cretans are liars."

If Epimenides' announcement is true, then he is lying because he is a Cretan, and what he has said is false. This is the "Liar Paradox." People lie for many diverse reasons. For example, we have all experienced "stretching the truth" in business situations for economic gain or business advantage.

People frequently lie for personal gain, and for personal aggrandizement. Sometimes, people tell "white lies" to be socially polite. Habitual liars have poor moral development, and no respect for the truth. There are also people who lie for amusement, as a personal hobby. Setting aside the moral implications, the intent, effect, and behavior resulting from the untruths are the essential factors for our workplace and personal interaction purposes.

EXAMPLE:

Amelia was an accomplished con artist. She thoroughly enjoyed lying for personal gain. She was proud of her ability to deceive people. She wanted a professional position that required specialized educational credentials. She didn't possess a medical degree, so she convincingly lied on her employment application and during the job interview process.

It wasn't that she couldn't handle the work. Amelia was highly intelligent and a quick study. She researched the needed skills on the Internet. She just lacked the appropriate educational credentials to be a psychiatrist.

For several years, no one noticed that Amelia was practicing medicine without a license. Her area of expertise was counseling "compulsive liars," and she was highly successful. Patients felt that she "truly understood" their problems. By State law, psychiatrists were required to complete twenty hours of Medical Continuing Education classes every two years. The classes were meant to protect patients by keeping practitioner medical knowledge current.

Amelia was employed as an independent contractor by a large private mental health facility. Because she was not a full-time employee, the facility had not been required to conduct a full background check on Amelia, but they were required to provide the appropriate Continuing Education classes as an employment benefit. Attendance was mandatory. At the end of each class, to receive credit, every participant completed a written form providing their professional license number. Amelia didn't have a medical license, so she wrote down a fake number.

When her employer submitted the forms for credit verification, Amelia's license number was reported as "incorrect." She was asked to verify a correct number. Amelia is no longer a practicing "psychiatrist," although she is still an expert on the subject of compulsive liars.

STRATEGIES FOR SUCCESS:

Even if it's not an absolute legal requirement, employers should conduct thorough, and independent, research to verify the truth, or falsehood, of factual statements. Although her status as an independent contractor may mitigate some liability due to the lack of background disclosure requirements, patients may have actionable claims against the facility resulting from Amelia's unauthorized practice. Always independently verify. If the "facts" are untrue, bring this to the attention of the individual for reasonable explanation. If there is no reasonable explanation (because it's a lie), then inform the group and take immediate appropriate action.

I AM ME ACTIVITY:

Liars usually have low self-esteem so they "invent" themselves. Practice good self-esteem by challenging the participants to tell the truth about themselves. Everyone has the opportunity to talk about themselves for three minutes. The challenge is that they must use the entire three minutes, and they cannot use the word "I"!

DISCUSSION IDEAS:

What creative ways did each person discover to involve the listener without directly using the word "I"? Did it get easier as the activity progressed because we heard other presentations? Did listening to "catch" the forbidden word make us pay better attention?

THIRTY FOUR

LIFE EXPERIENCE

"To find out what is truly individual in ourselves, profound reflection is needed; and suddenly we realize how uncommonly difficult the discovery of individuality is." ~ C.G. Jung

Humanistic psychology, pioneered by Abraham Maslow, theorizes that we are all motivated by the universal human need to be fulfilled and "self-actualized." Having the psychological freedom "to become everything that one is capable of becoming" creates peace with others and within ourselves. Subjective life experiences form human nature. Life experiences not only fuel personal growth and self-realization, they shape how we deal with new situations, and other people. Everyone brings their personal history, and goals for the future, with them to the negotiation table. The more life experience, the more opinionated and certain of the correct course people can become.

Though we hear the U.S. Army ads boast that we all strive to "become the best that we can be," personal fulfillment takes many forms, and is often difficult, leading to frustration that manifests itself in uncooperative behavior.

EXAMPLE:

Liam did not like people. He especially did not like groups of people. He considered himself to be an "individualist." He certainly wasn't interested in whatever anyone else thought. He always knew what needed to be done, and he always knew exactly how to do it — whatever "it" was.

Liam was employed as an onsite technician for a large cable company. He received daily assignments via email, and visited client workplaces to perform necessary repairs. He loved his job, and he enjoyed working alone in the field. Because of his high client satisfaction rating, Liam was promoted to area supervisor. His new job required team training, employee supervision, and people management skills. Liam needed to create working groups, a prospect that annoyed him because it involved too much human interaction, which meant too many people with stupid opinions.

Liam considered mentoring instead of group creation, but there were too many employees in his "area" to train individually. There were also too many skill levels. Some employees were new to the job; others were experienced but needed to refresh their skills. All of them, including Liam, needed to earn "re-certification" credits for fieldwork. Group participation and training was the only option.

Liam was certain that he knew exactly what to do. The correct technique was obvious. He would carefully explain his past experiences in the field, and everyone else would have to listen, agree, and absorb this information. After all, he knew best. To his surprise, Liam realized that everyone else in the group was also an "individualist." That's why they all enjoyed the autonomy of fieldwork. They had different experiences to share. They had different, but not adverse, opinions.

Liam was still skeptical, but group participants were required to actively participate and take turns speaking. They were forced to listen to each other. Upon discussion and reflection, some original viewpoints were modified. Even Liam was forced to modify his original viewpoint concerning the concept of "group participation" as an effective management tool. They shared knowledge, past mistakes as well as successes, and lessons learned from on-the-job experience. The primary group focus was practical knowledge, not esoteric theory. Everyone agreed that group participation was a valuable resource, and they all successfully completed their re-certification requirements.

STRATEGIES FOR SUCCESS:

Recognize and acknowledge that although the "path" may be complicated, the ultimate outcome will be worth the effort. Liam had prior life experience indicating that group participation was frustrating and useless, creating negative expectations. Group members, especially those required to attend as an employment expectation, often feel like Liam. Prevent frustration with the process from overwhelming the participants. Allow for personal and professional growth by valuing life experience and encouraging active group participation.

EXPERIENCE IN COMMON ACTIVITY:

Divide large groups into teams of four to eight participants. The teams will be issued pads of paper and will designate a team leader to take notes and report back to the group as a whole. Give them fifteen minutes to make a list of experiences the team members have in common, and those experiences they do not share. To be included on the "common" list, the experiences must be something outside the obvious such as attending this seminar or working in the same business.

DISCUSSION IDEAS:

When we re-assembled the entire group, what experiences did we have in common? What experiences were the least common?

THIRTY FIVE

LOGICISM

"The difference between the right word, and the almost right word, is the difference between lightning and the lightning bug." ~ Mark Twain

Sometimes, it's possible to over-think an argument, and create a false "logical" conclusion. For example, German mathematician, logician and philosopher Friedrich Frege attempted to define all mathematical concepts and prove all mathematical truths using only principles of logic in the late 19th century. It seemed like a reasonable concept. Mathematics is a straightforward science that appears to be capable of logical proof.

Frege's mathematical version of "logicism" was surprisingly unsuccessful. What he did prove was that it is possible to overthink even mathematical conclusions, and create false logic.

Bertrand Russell applied logicism principles to sentence structure. He argued that every sentence has a "logical form" which makes its meaning and logic clearly understood.

Russell proposed that the reference of a sentence is its meaning. He uses as an example the phrase "the present King of France." This phrase has no meaning by itself, but can be translated into a sentence in which the phrase doesn't occur. "The present King of France is bald" becomes "There is one and only one present King of France, and he is bald."

Russell argued that the second sentence revealed the logical form of the first sentence. Do you agree? Why does it make a difference? Whenever presented with a complex series of issues, we need to approach solutions in a logical manner. Instead of attempting to tackle them all at once, divide the thought process into a series of logical interconnected steps. Each step will then be capable of resolution before progressing forward up the "staircase" to the next issue.

EXAMPLE:

Sarah was an attorney, but she considered herself to be a linguistic philosopher. She loved both writing and logically interpreting legal documents. She wrote in long, complicated sentences deliberately using obscure words whenever possible. Her legal documents harkened back to a time when lawyers got paid by the word. Sarah felt that her legal writings were beautiful and scholarly. Her colleagues felt that her writings were pompous and obtuse.

Sarah was hired to write a contract agreement for the purchase of a large United States software company by a multi-national corporation. It was a substantial monetary investment requiring government approval and official documents. The purchaser was primarily interested in acquiring all legal rights to the seller's software technology. The seller was primarily interested in acquiring the purchaser's money. The negotiated agreement was not simple, but it was straightforward. Sarah made it complicated. Instead of using logical form, Sarah crafted a seventy-five page document filled with beautiful, old fashioned, verbiage obscuring the intent of the parties. She enjoyed writing it.

When a disagreement concerning the terms of the sale arose, each side interpreted the document in their favor. The exact same sentences were used to bolster opposite arguments. The parties went to arbitration. The arbitrator couldn't positively decipher the contract terms contained in the documents. Logical form was impossible to determine from the wording.

Sarah was summoned to assist in the interpretation. She didn't remember the original intent of the parties, and she was forced to admit that her writing was unclear.

The parties eventually reached a negotiated agreement. They had it memorialized in logical form by an attorney who was not a "linguistic philosopher." Sarah retired from the active practice of law, and became a law school professor.

STRATEGIES FOR SUCCESS:

Philosophers and linguists, including Noam Chomsky and Ludwig Wittgenstein, have endorsed Russell's logicism theories. Although Sarah thought that her writing was a clear representation of the agreement, she needed to re-read the document from the viewpoint of an impartial third-party judge. Even she couldn't decipher the details after a period of time had elapsed! Precise sentence construction becomes important and is often a contentious issue when interpreting laws, rules, and regulations. Precise wording and attention to logical sentence construction are essential when writing proposals and formal documents. Logicism principles create a gold standard for clear interpretation of all written communication.

PUZZLE LOGIC ACTIVITY:

Practice working as a group using logic to construct a puzzle picture. Divide the group into teams of four and issue each team a different but equally difficult set of jigsaw puzzle pieces. Jumble the pieces and do not divulge the completed puzzle picture so that the participants must work together to logically assemble the pieces by color and shape. This activity can be simplified (and speeded up) by using children's puzzles although I prefer to create a challenge with "easy" level adult jigsaws.

DISCUSSION IDEAS:

Why were some participants faster at solving the puzzle? Did everyone on the team participate equally? What was the progression of logical "steps" in assembling the puzzle pieces?

THIRTY SIX

MEMES

"There are nine and sixty ways of constructing tribal lays, and every single one of them is right." ~ Rudyard Kipling

Everyone copies, emulates, and modifies ideas and behavior modeled by respected authority figures within their culture. Richard Dawkins created the term "meme" to describe this replication and modification of cultural lessons that are then passed-on for replication and modification by the next generation.

The term "meme" has also been used by contemporary marketing and advertising experts to indicate a symbol or spokesperson that represents a company. Think of the Target corporation red bull's-eye, or the Starbucks mermaid.

Most memes are not marketing icons. They are helpful foundations for dealing with everyday life. Some memes are less beneficial, and adversely shape our worldview and our ability to successfully deal with "outsiders."

EXAMPLE:

Lucas greatly admired his grandfather who had been a famous and highly regarded Faith Healer. He had, as a child, watched the faith-healing miracles and knew that his family was touched by the blessings of God.

Grandfather not only preached the healing of all physical and spiritual ailments through the power of prayer, he could actually "lay hands" on the afflicted person, and they would frequently be healed. If the person remained afflicted, they were deemed to lack the required level of faith. If children too young to have spiritual understanding remained afflicted, their parents were deemed lacking in the necessary level of faith to save them.

Lucas was a man of deep faith. Whenever he was sick, he turned to prayer, and was cured of his affliction. He personally rejected medical science as "an abomination against the powers of God as healer of the faithful." When his son became afflicted with cancer, Lucas turned to prayer and rejected medical science. He emulated the habits, skills, stories, songs, prayers and mannerisms of his grandfather when treating his son. He enlisted the assistance of respected faith healers. The cancer was spreading. Lucas was certain that it wasn't because of insufficient faith. His son's school called social services. Medical care was court mandated. In response, Lucas hid his son from the authorities.

Before the situation could escalate into criminal proceedings, the Hospital Chaplain explained to Lucas that medical procedures do not preclude the power of prayer; they are symbiotic. In fact, they would prayer together over his son during his hospital stay. Lucas, the hospital chaplain, friends, family members, and faith healers came to the hospital to offer prayers of healing. Their prayers, in combination with medical science, were effective.

STRATEGIES FOR SUCCESS:

Lucas had been profoundly influenced by his foundational example of Faith Healing. His core meme was personified by his Grandfather; a man who had taken on larger-than-life proportions. Although outsiders unfavorably interpreted his behavior and its logical consequences, Lucas was not being unreasonable, and he was not deliberately risking his son's life. He was acting in accordance with a foundational cultural belief so pervasive that it had become a meme. Respectfully acknowledge the cultural meme. Create a reasonable basis for allowing the individual to accept an "outsider" viewpoint for this specific situation without requiring that the foundational meme be compromised.

PERCEPTION ACTIVITY:

Misunderstandings often occur because our assumptions or perceptions are inaccurate due to categorically applying a cultural meme. Divide into groups of six and instruct the participants to take five-minute turns non-verbally showing the group an activity that they enjoy. Similar to the game of Charades, the audience is allowed to ask questions but the actor must use non-verbal clues.

DISCUSSION IDEAS:

Why were some non-verbal clues harder than others? Were the questions influenced by participant assumptions and perceptions of the activities they enjoyed? Did some activities defy understanding and require disclosure after the five minutes were up?

THIRTY SEVEN

MORAL STAGES

"If the chief party, whether it be the people, or the army, or the nobility, which you think most useful and of most consequence to you for the conservation of your dignity, be corrupt, you must follow their humor and indulge them, and in that case honesty and virtue are pernicious." ~ Machiavelli

Moral development is a life-long process. Research psychologist Lawrence Kohlberg studied moral development from childhood to adulthood, concluding that there are six developmental stages. Stages one through four involve moral development during childhood. By Stage Five, adult humans understand that although moral rules exist and should be followed, individual needs must also be considered.

At the highest level, Stage Six, behavior is determined by self-chosen moral principles established through conscious reflection, such as justice and respect. Adherence to these moral principles creates moral responsibility. According to Dr. Kohlberg, many people never fully achieve Stage Six.

EXAMPLE:

Ruby was an extremely successful pension fund manager. Unfortunately, she had not achieved Stage Six of Dr. Kohlberg's moral development theory. Although Ruby knew that she behaved in a manner indicating a complete lack of moral responsibility, she experienced no shame. She was proud of her aggressive nature, and considered it to be an important business asset.

She deliberately ignored all rules of conduct that didn't directly benefit her financially. Ruby perceived no financial advantages to morality. Ruby understood that other people possessed personal codes of moral conduct. She referred to these people as "suckers," and tried to take advantage of their business "weakness."

Some of these "suckers" were her pension fund clients. They invested money with Ruby in good faith that the money was being properly handled. They felt confident investing because Ruby was a licensed, and highly recommended, financial planner with client fiduciary duties.

In violation of her fiduciary responsibilities, Ruby had created a "shell" investment vehicle to automatically siphon client funds into her personal offshore bank account. The pension funds had been deliberately defrauded. The client money was missing, and so was Ruby. Her now former clients weren't happy.

The defrauded pension funds belonged to multinational corporations who cooperated in the fraud investigation. The combined amount of stolen money was substantial, and the corporations wanted restitution.

An international cooperative law enforcement effort located both Ruby and her bank account by tracing her numerous credit card transactions. Criminal charges were filed, and the money was recovered. Ruby now writes investment advice books from prison. She still lacks Stage Six moral development. Her only regret is "being busted." What Dr. Martin Luther King calls the *11th Commandment*: "Thou shalt not get caught."

STRATEGIES FOR SUCCESS:

We, of course, have strong moral principles. The same cannot be said for everyone else. Emotional factors such as greed, lust for control or power, and fear of failure impact the level of perceived moral responsibility. Ruby internally justified her actions as aggressively proper business decisions. In the short term, she was financially successful, so she justified continued activities. In the long term, she ran afoul of externalized rules of moral conduct created by public laws, and was punished. Ruby knew better. She understood both the moral and legal implications, deliberately choosing to ignore them. Did the punishment cause her to reach Stage Six of moral development? People like Ruby cannot be forced into morality, but they can be forced out of business.

Kohlberg claimed that approximately ten percent of adults reached Stage Six in their moral development. This means that 90% of the population never achieves the highest level, and they're our participants. Remember to consider not only the issues of the dispute, but the moral character of everyone involved, and the repercussions of their behavior.

WHAT IF ACTIVITY:

Present the group with a hypothetical business dilemma where one solution will be economically unfavorable, and the economically favorable solution is not technically illegal but will cause economic hardship to someone else.

DISCUSSION IDEAS:

How can we determine what is moral? Are there differences between personal moral character and business morals? Who decides?

THIRTY EIGHT

NARCISSISM

"A man wrapped up in himself makes a very small bundle." ~ Benjamin Franklin

The mythological Narcissus fell in love with his own reflection. He became so obsessed with his own beauty that he died of starvation, unable to think of anything but his image. In contemporary psychology, narcissism is extreme self-adoration. The person may not starve to death like Narcissus, but it is more than vanity, pride, or self-confidence.

True narcissists can appear to be charming at first glance. However, they lack human empathy. Narcissists always consider themselves to be the most wonderful, charming, intelligent person in the room. Rarely do they hear even a loud hint to the contrary.

EXAMPLE:

By his estimation, Alexander believed he was perfect. His absolute perfection was obvious to anyone who knew him. His physical appearance and personal style were perfect. Alexander couldn't pass by a mirror without admiring his own reflection. His fantastically wonderful personality was perfect, too. He was truly a superior human being in every possible way.

Because he was perfect (and his father owned the company), Alexander was appointed to a managerial position where his perfect ideas were always important. Disagreement by lesser human beings would not be tolerated.

Because they were practical business people who needed to find workable solutions, the other managers didn't always think that Alexander was perfect. They frequently disagreed with his imaginative but unrealistic ideas. Fortunately for the economic wellbeing of the company, Alexander needed lots of physical pampering during business hours. He frequented luxurious spas, high-end tailors and beauty salons instead of business meetings.

Alexander knew that his perfectly beautiful image functioned as a corporate beacon among the boring grey suits of the other managers. They were unworthy compared to him. He couldn't be bothered with tedious meetings full of tedious people having tedious ideas. His ideas were always fantastic.

Each member of the corporate management team thought Alexander's ideas were not fantastic, but fantastical. They were neither economically feasible nor possible to legally implement. Still, because he was the president's son, Alexander frequently received praise for his ideas, and was awarded beautiful company commendations to hang on his office wall. From a practical business perspective Alexander was harmless although rather annoying. The commendations kept Alexander happy, and the company was saved from his perfection.

STRATEGIES FOR SUCCESS:

We've all known and been annoyed by narcissists. Alexander is obviously insecure and concerned about his physical appearance. But he is also insecure about his professional stature which manifests itself in his attention craving behavior. Even the slightest public humoring will satisfy the craving for attention and appreciation. For example, narcissists love feeling superior by winning awards. Displaying the award will often fixate the narcissistic behavior on the object, providing a source of pride, and relief from the need for constant affirmation by colleagues.

APPEARANCE ACTIVITY:

Even people who are not narcissists are susceptible to first impressions based upon superficial appearances. Divide the group into teams of four and give each group the same four photographs of different types of people. Participants will have ten minutes to discuss their first impressions of the people in the photos based solely upon their physical appearance. Each team will record these impressions and then report back to the group as a whole.

DISCUSSION IDEAS:

Was there consensus amongst the teams? Were there gender differences in judgments? Did team members compromise their first impressions after group discussion?

THIRTY NINE

OBEDIENCE TO AUTHORITY

"The world is not dangerous because of those who do harm, but because of those who look at it without doing anything" ~ Albert Einstein

Within the history of Nazi Germany one can find ordinary citizens and soldiers acting in a manner that was contrary to reasonable standards of human behavior. Under extraordinarily insane and cruel totalitarian governments found in many parts of the world, we can still find shocking capitulation to the status quo.

Studies show that obedience to an authority figure influences extreme behavior. This occurs even if the "authority" is temporary, and without the threat of dire repercussions for disobedience.

As was described in Chapter 23, psychologist Stanley Milgram published his own Obedience Study. He offered us a classic example of ordinary human beings with ordinary values of decency — people deemed "normal" — asked to volunteer for what they understood to be a "memory" study. The volunteers believed that they were controlling electric shocks as punishment for wrong answers given by a strapped-down participant. As the session progressed, the strapped-down participant (who was an actor, and not actually in danger) screamed and begged as the volunteer controlling the electric shocks believed that they were administering higher and higher voltages.

When the actor "scientist" merely stood in the corner of the room and instructed the volunteers with phrases such as "the experiment requires that you continue," 65% of the volunteers delivered what they believed to be lethal shocks. The percentage of those willing to kill their fellow volunteer for the inability to remember question answers increased when others in the room were also willing to obey.

Frequently, the people we are dealing with have consulted with an authority figure. They have asked for advice, for guidance, and for instruction. They have been told how to proceed. The authority figure monitors their progress, giving further advice. There's a "scientist" standing in the corner hindering compromise, preventing a reasonable outcome.

EXAMPLE:

Georgia didn't understand what had changed. Her business partner was being uncharacteristically unreasonable. He and Georgia had been business partners for more than 15 years, and they were a highly successful team. Both of them had always acted in a professional and reasonable manner towards each other, until now.

There had been differences of opinion over the years, but they had always discussed any problems and agreed upon a successful compromise. They had always been great business partners, and great friends.

Suddenly, it was as though her partner's personality, his perspective, and his ability to be reasonable had all become impaired. The question was: "Why?" Georgia took a direct approach, and asked what was "different." She discovered that her partner had a new "life coach." The coach informed him that his "life problems" were caused by his being too agreeable and too willing to compromise.

Georgia acknowledged that a life coach could be a valid consultant. She listened seriously, and without judgment, to the advice that her partner had been given. After sympathetic private discussion and serious contemplation, they decided that being able to reasonably negotiate, and reach compromise, was a good business approach. They decided that the life coach would approve.

STRATEGIES FOR SUCCESS:

Throughout our lives, we all follow the example and advice of people we've come to respect. Georgia's partner hired a professional without considering whether or not their advice was worthy of respect. The advice was too general (barely more than a newspaper horoscope prediction), and it was taken too literally. Without being judgmental, Georgia modified her partner's obedience to authority. Politely, to prevent embarrassment or misunderstanding of your good intentions, ask if anyone else has been consulted. Indicate respect for the authority figure, ask what has been advised, and work on a mutually acceptable solution.

INFLUENCE ACTIVITY:

Obedience to authority is not necessarily negative. The authority figure might be a positive role model. Participants have three minutes to tell about the person who was their greatest influence. If participants prefer not to discuss a personal authority figure, the influencer can be historical, mythical, or even a hypothetical composite created from varied life experiences.

DISCUSSION IDEAS:

What traits do positive authority figures have in common? Are role models always authority figures? How important are negative role models who show us what not to do?

FORTY

OCKHAM'S RAZOR

"I do believe in simplicity. It is astonishing as well as sad, how many trivial affairs even the wisest thinks he must attend to in a day; how singular an affair he thinks he must omit. When the mathematician would solve a difficult problem, he first frees the equation of all encumbrances, and reduces it to its simplest terms. So simplify the problem of life, distinguish the necessary and the real. Probe the earth to see where your main roots run." ~ Henry David Thoreau

The medieval philosopher and logician William of Ockham noticed that "elegant explanations" are more likely to be successful than convoluted ones. The term "elegant" is not necessarily synonymous with the word "simple," it means free of Thoreau's "encumbrances."

Ockham was neither the first, nor the last, philosopher to advocate making the fewest number of assumptions necessary to reach a conclusion. He is famous for using a metaphorical "razor" to remove unnecessary excess.

The ancient philosopher Ptolemy is regarded as the first to notice that: "We consider it a good principle to explain phenomena by the simplest hypothesis possible." We often become entangled in the myriad of minutia surrounding an issue. The simple explanation, the simple solution, the most straightforward idea, is sometimes the best choice.

EXAMPLE:

Jayden disliked "elegant explanations." He favored complicated solutions that took months to implement. He was delighted by, and encouraged, his clients to engage in adversarial and unnecessarily complicated negotiations.

Jayden was a well-paid professional negotiation consultant employed by a mediation services company. He was paid an hourly fee, and his employer greatly encouraged extending the negotiations as long as possible. Jayden, and his employer, understood that when the problems were resolved, his services were no longer needed. They were not advocates of Ockham's "Razor" theory.

Jayden also enjoyed the negotiation process. He felt disappointed when issues were resolved and there were no more meetings and committee reports. The clients favored "elegant explanations." They always wanted to find the simplest solution, in the fastest manner, and get on with business. Because the clients valued speed and simplicity, essential details were often glossed-over and ignored. The clients and the mediation services company recognized the need to resolve their competing interests in an equitable manner.

Balance was needed. An advisory committee, including the client management team and the negotiation consultants, was formed. Impartial third-party research was gathered. All solutions and ideas were carefully considered in an efficient and time sensitive manner.

The negotiations were thorough, without becoming convoluted. After considering a combination of several ideas and opinions, they decided the final, and correct approach was the simplest one.

STRATEGIES FOR SUCCESS:

Often, issues are complex and necessary decisions are made by a committee. Recognizing the correct "simple" choice is easier-said-than-done, especially when there is more than one "correct" answer. If Jayden is the committee Chairperson, the process will become convoluted and frustrating to all participants (except Jayden). The key is to examine the underlying assumptions so that we can successfully create a foundation upon which to build. What could be eliminated? Is there redundant complexity? Why?

Often, there is no single simple solution. The negotiation process requires a series of steps to unravel issue complexity, and ultimately achieve a successful outcome. Think of the steps as a stairway, with each step a logical progression from the last one. Once a decision has been made, move on to the next step.

STORY BY COMMITTEE ACTIVITY:

A simple project can become convoluted if too many people add a single word — like cooks in a kitchen. Allow enough time so that the entire group can create a story by taking turns adding the next word until the story is completed or the time runs out. In smaller groups, everyone gets more than one turn. For example, participants start the story with different people adding each of the words "once," "upon," "a," "time," "my," "business," "partner"…

DISCUSSION IDEAS:

Is this an elegant way to create a story? Was there a logical progression or did the story lose focus? Did we lose control of the storyline in our desperation to choose the next word?

FORTY ONE

ODYSSEUS

"What lies in our power to do, it lies in our power not to do." ~ Aristotle

The great mythical hero Odysseus was famous for his cunning in battle. He invented the wooden Trojan Horse, which was filled with warriors, as a battlefield tactic to end the siege of Troy. He was also renowned for his successful negotiation tactics. For example, after serious and somewhat deceptive negotiation, the Phaeacians provided him with ships for his journey home.

Odysseus is also the quintessential example of manipulative business practices. He employed lies and deception to achieve his results. Because he was an ancient God-like mythical hero, his deceptions were justified as "cunning." Contemporary negotiation tactics prohibit deception. In the contemporary era, many of his actions would incur civil and criminal liability. Corporate ethical standards are not just good business they are mandated by law. Deception is not a Godlike activity, it is legally actionable and fiduciary responsibility is taken very seriously by the courts.

EXAMPLE:

The corporate CEO prided himself on being a "straight-arrow." He was honest, plain spoken, and without guile. The company was in the machine tool business. Machine tools need to be not only well constructed and reliable, they also need to be the right tool for the job. On a personal level, the CEO didn't really like Emma, his most successful salesperson, but he did like the woman's ability to sell machine tools. Business was important, and Emma brought in a substantial amount of business.

The biggest competitors in the machine tool industry complained about Emma to her CEO. They implied that her business practices were deceptive, contending that Emma would dishonestly convince customers to purchase unnecessary tools. The CEO understood that competitors are always complaining. However, he reported the competitor concerns to Emma.

Emma convinced the CEO that her competitors were merely jealous of her success. The CEO believed Emma, and was satisfied with her explanation. He did not authorize an internal corporate investigation into the allegations. The competitors complained to the authorities. An investigation revealed that Emma, as an inducement to purchase unnecessary additional products, was paying Inventory Supervisors bribes in the form of overcharging the customer company and then "kicking back" the excess amount to the Supervisor when the order contract was signed.

The Attorney General filed charges. The investigation was thorough, and Emma was found guilty. The court levied a substantial corporate penalty because Emma was acting as an agent for the company, and the company had been previously notified of the deceptive practices. The CEO incurred a great deal of legal expense, and bad publicity, attempting to prove his innocence of personal wrongdoing.

STRATEGIES FOR SUCCESS:

Ultimately, in both the workplace and personal life, dishonesty never pays. Although Emma was the actual perpetrator, the CEO in our example was equally culpable because he was aware of the situation, had the power and the obligation to control it, but decided to do nothing. Since none of us are mythical heroes like Odysseus, cunning and deception have no place in our process. It should be made clear that deceptive practices will not be tolerated. Set clear guidelines for compliance, with appropriate, and swiftly enforced, sanctions for violations. Regularly scheduled internal audit procedures should be mandated.

FRAUD EXPERIENCE ACTIVITY:

Allow two minutes for each participant to describe a fraudulent or deceptive experience. If they prefer not to relate a personal experience, suggest the use of a recent incident reported in the media or a hypothetical event.

DISCUSSION IDEAS:

What action did they take and what was the result? Did anyone get offered a bribe, and what did they do about it? Discuss the experience similarities and the differing results depending upon the chosen action.

FORTY TWO

PEER PRESSURE

"Keep away from people who try to belittle your ambitions. Small people always do that, but the really great make you feel that you, too, can become great." ~ Mark Twain

Peer pressure occurs when a person is unduly influenced by the opinions and behaviors of his/her peer group. Peer pressure, combined with systemic circumstances, can create uncharacteristic individual behavior. You certainly don't have to be a teenager to succumb to "group think."

The "Stanford Prison Experiment" studied prison dynamics using volunteer groups as both mock guards and mock prisoners. Both groups were evaluated beforehand and deemed emotionally stable. Due to the influence of peer pressure, the experiment was abandoned halfway through its scheduled time period. The experiment ended because a substantial percentage of the "guards" were behaving sadistically to the "prisoners."

The research findings indicated that the "guards" engaged in "pornographic and degrading abuse." Equally unexpected, instead of taking appropriate action and ending the brutality, a substantial percentage of the "prisoners" became distraught and submissive.

Peer pressure isn't confined to school children or test subjects. Any situation with social, cultural, or economic peer groups creates pressure to conform. When this pressure turns negative, problems result.

☾

EXAMPLE:

Jacob prided himself on his self-control. He was cautious, conservative, and strictly followed all rules and regulations. Because Jacob was such a "straight arrow," his co-workers enjoyed taunting him. He was constantly subjected to annoying and juvenile workplace behavior. Jacob never reported the inappropriate behavior, or retaliated. Encouraged by his lack of response, the taunting escalated.

The week before Valentine's Day, the office supervisor asked an attractive young female intern to make-a-play for Jacob. Mistakenly, he assumed that she was sincerely interested in a personal relationship, and he responded with inappropriate touching. The "joke" was videotaped and posted on the Internet. Management noticed the situation when the intern filed a sexual harassment complaint. The supervisor insisted that the incident was a practical joke. He contended that everyone in the office had fully understood the situation, and that the woman had agreed to participate. "Everyone knew" that Jacob was "fair game."

The video graphically depicted the attempted physical touching of a young intern by a full-time staff member. There was no indication that the video was a pre-planned practical joke. The intern appeared to be distraught and offended on-screen. The amount of the negotiated settlement wasn't funny.

STRATEGIES FOR SUCCESS:

Unfortunately, we don't outgrow peer pressure when we leave high school; sometimes adults in the workplace — especially those with low self-esteem — are more susceptible to its influence. We spend our business and personal lives living in groups of various sizes, and the other group members become our "peers." Those members with the greatest confidence, often indicated by stature within the group, become the leaders. The leaders are also subject to "peer pressure," and the group members as a whole must prevent group leaders from becoming the "guards" and bullying the others into negative behavior. Listen to reports of abuse and take immediate action. Be sensitive to the formation of sub-groups wielding disproportionate influence.

WORD PRESSURE ACTIVITY:

Whenever we engage in group competition, peer pressure comes into play. Divide the group into two teams and issue each team the same crossword puzzle. The teams have ten minutes to complete the crossword puzzle with the winning team winning a bag of candy sufficient to share with the entire group.

DISCUSSION IDEAS:

Was there pressure within the team to correctly complete the puzzle? What happened if someone made a wrong suggestion? What happened if someone knew a difficult answer? Did all team members equally participate or were there dominant players? Did the winning team share the prize candy with the entire group, or only with their teammates?

FORTY THREE

PHAETHON

"The one who knows all the answers has not been asked all the questions."
~ Confucius

The mythical Phaethon was the son of Helios, the Greek God who drove the sun across the sky in his chariot every morning. Phaethon questioned his immortal paternity because his mother was married to a mortal king. In an effort to prove his paternity, Helios promised Phaethon anything that he desired. The chariot was created for the God to carry the light of day, so of course the son wanted to drive it!

Phaethon lost control of the chariot when the divine horses refused to obey him. The chariot carried the heat of the sun, which was now out of control, placing the earth in danger. Zeus, leader of the Gods, kills Phaethon with a thunderbolt to prevent the impending disaster. This ancient story is, of course, a morals-tale exemplifying the modern day saying: "Be careful what you wish for."

EXAMPLE:

Madison had invented a new type of recreational vehicle completely wired for Internet gaming connections. The vehicle Internet capability was strong enough to work even in the most remote recreational areas. There was even a connection and large screen embedded in the dashboard area so that the driver and front seat passenger could engage in multi-player competition. It was revolutionary.

Madison needed funding for commercial production. She created a proto-type and a funding proposal detailing the vehicle schematics as well as projected production costs.

Anticipated market share was substantial. The prototype was rated "awesome" by all of the most respected gaming websites.

A major automobile manufacturer expressed interest in producing the vehicle and purchasing the patents. They convened a committee of engineers and marketing experts to analyze the proposal and the estimated market potential. They wanted to approve. They wanted something "awesome." Their consumer demographic was 45-55 years old. They needed to increase revenue and market futuristic products appealing to younger drivers in order to stay competitive.

The committee considered the excessive manufacturing cost, which would necessitate an excessive consumer list price. The committee discussed the unknown market potential because none had actually been produced and sold. Most importantly, the committee discussed the need to modify the original schematics. It was clear, from a liability perspective, that a vehicle capable of being driven on public roadways could not have the driver actively engaged in a multi-player game while driving. They brought in experts to determine if changing the schematics would reduce the "awesome" quotient. They created test groups to determine the opinions of consumers in a younger demographic.

They consulted with experts in the gaming community. They consulted with marketing experts. They made financial projections. After careful consideration, they decided that although the vehicle was indeed awesome, it was not a good "fit" for the company.

The committee understood that although the company wished to successfully navigate future trends, this specific vehicle did not fulfill that desire. They declined the proposal.

STRATEGIES FOR SUCCESS:

Be careful what you wish for. Decisions and products need to be a good "fit" within the business culture. From the top of power to the bottom, everyone grows by experiencing limitations. Madison's product was "awesome," but the company needed to be realistic without being unduly pessimistic concerning their future potential. Committees, because of the diverse personalities inherent in their make-up, are especially prone to wishful thinking. Before deciding on a recommended course of action, determine if the recommendation is practical, reasonable, and capable of accomplishment under the circumstances.

WE'VE COME A LONG WAY ACTIVITY:

When the group must decide on a new course of action, using a visual aid assists the process by creating a focused reference point. As a group activity, create a timeline to reflect group past successes and their intentions toward future success. If appropriate, include ideas and recommendations that had been considered but not adopted and decide as a group whether or not circumstances have changed and they should be re-considered.

DISCUSSION IDEAS:

How was success defined? What does future success look like? How should we determine which ideas warrant re-consideration?

FORTY FOUR

THE PLACEBO EFFECT

"Get your facts first, and then you can distort them as much as you please"
~ Mark Twain

We've all heard of the "placebo effect" in reference to evidence based medicine trials and research. To test the effectiveness of a trial drug, patients are divided into two groups in a "randomized controlled trial." One group receives the medication, and the other group receives an inert look-alike (the placebo). Effectiveness of the drug, as opposed to the placebo, is then measured.

Major medical studies from recognized research organizations, including the Mayo Clinic, have shown that placebos are often deemed "effective" by the trial participants. The pill size, the color of the medication, and the attitude of the person administering the placebo all increase the likelihood of a positive patient response.

The "placebo effect" is really the power of suggestion. When we believe that something is an excellent choice, we also believe that it will be beneficial. In negotiation strategy, alternative solutions can create a "face saving" effect, even if the actual benefits are minimal.

EXAMPLE:

The volunteer team had worked very hard. People were dying of malaria all over the world, and they needed to raise funds for medical assistance and mosquito netting. Everyone had put in many extra hours of their own time. They were kind-hearted, charitable people, and dedicated to the cause. The grant proposal had been competently and professionally presented. Despite all of their efforts, the proposal was rejected, and they would not be receiving the desperately needed funds.

Luke was the charity Executive Director. He had spearheaded the attempted fundraising. He felt just as dejected as everyone else. On a practical level, he was even more dejected because he was no longer being paid. He realized that they needed a team-building, morale booster to re-invigorate enthusiasm. They needed to win. The team needed a fundraising success. They needed to feel that it wasn't hopeless. They needed a project grant, even if the actual funds were minimal.

Luke contacted his brother who was a wealthy neurosurgeon involved in many charitable foundations, and explained the desperate nature of the situation. His brother agreed to make a generous donation to an important grant making foundation with the understanding that the foundation would approve a small grant to the malaria charity.

The actual amount of grant money was minimal. It wasn't sufficient to purchase, and ship, either medication or mosquito netting in significant amounts. However, receiving a grant from a well-known foundation renewed enthusiasm. They promoted receiving the grant on their website, in marketing materials, and when writing new grant proposals. Other funding sources were impressed by the foundation grant, and additional contributions were successfully solicited. They were able to continue their good works, and Luke was able to continue as a paid Executive Director.

STRATEGIES FOR SUCCESS:

Luke understood the psychological value of a perceived success. Receiving the grant not only energized his own team, it encouraged outside additional donations because the charity was favorably perceived as a "winner." Are we recommending falsely inducing success by creating a fake solution? Of course not! Luke did not *fake a solution*; he received a legitimate grant to "start the ball rolling."

Grant-funding foundations prefer to donate their funds to projects that have already shown promise. If you have won one grant, you're more likely to receive another. Everybody wants to back a winner.

Stagnation can also occur during the negotiation process. The participants need to successfully negotiate a small issue so that the larger issues can be resolved. Developing a placebo issue, and resolving it to everyone's satisfaction, will generate renewed enthusiasm to move the process forward.

AGREE TO CELEBRATE ACTIVITY:

The purpose of a placebo is to encourage the group and make everyone feel better. A hypothetical placebo issue can be created and satisfactorily resolved, but it's often easier and more fulfilling to remember to celebrate the small successes as they occur. The celebration should be a fun group treat and deliberately emphasize that each small success adds up to greater accomplishment. The goal is to sustain enthusiasm and move forward.

DISCUSSION IDEAS:

How should we define a success worthy of celebration? What would the group choose as an activity to celebrate our latest success? Should we track our successes over a three-month period and then have a larger cumulative celebration?

FORTY FIVE

PLATO'S CAVE

"Through pride we are ever deceiving ourselves. But deep down below the surface of the average conscience a still, small voice says to us, something is out of tune." ~ C.G. Jung

In Plato's Cave — also known as the *Allegory of the Cave* — he starts the story with Socrates teaching a gathering of people who have lived chained to the wall of a cave all of their lives, facing a blank wall. The people watch shadows projected on the wall by things passing in front of a fire behind them, and begin to ascribe forms to these shadows. According to Plato's Socrates, the shadows are as close as the prisoners can get to *seeing* reality. He makes the connection between the philosopher and the prisoner who is freed from the cave and comes to understand that the shadows on the wall do not make up reality at all. When chained to one particular view of things, they can't see how things work outside the cave of their limited thinking.[4] They believe that the shadows are the only reality, and have passed this belief from generation to generation as "fact."

If one cave dweller ventured outside into the light, he would be initially blinded. Eventually, he would look around and see the true reality. He would see the Sun giving light. When he returned to the cave, the others in the group became threatened and refused to believe his revelations. No longer would he be allowed to live.

Plato's Cave is, of course, a metaphor. The cave dwellers are the stubbornly ignorant majority. The adventurer is a philosopher who discovers the sun illuminating truth. The death of the philosopher represents the execution of Socrates.

---

[4] "Allegory of the Cave," *The Republic*, Plato (514a-520a).

How is Plato's Cave relevant today? Groups still refuse to see the Sun. They ostracize (hopefully not kill) any member who deviates from the group's "factual" beliefs and discovers new ideas.

EXAMPLE:

Harrison loved tradition. He loved everything old-fashioned, and often lamented that he was born in the wrong era. He would have been much happier living during the Renaissance.

His friends all felt the same way. They were Renaissance Men trapped in an unspeakable modern world. They needed a place where they could be comfortable and indulge themselves, so they formed a private members-only Renaissance club.

They all agreed that it was a fantastic idea, but they had a problem. Private clubs catering to renaissance tastes are extraordinarily expensive to create and maintain. Unfortunately, they were not fabulously wealthy men.

Harrison, being the most progressive member of the group, recommended hiring a professional consulting firm to determine what needed to be done. The consultants advised holding a membership drive to attract new members with new money. Harrison thought it was a great idea. He loved meeting new people who shared his passion for the Renaissance, and he wanted the club to prosper.

The other club members disagreed; they didn't like outsiders and couldn't agree on membership criteria. Nobody could possibly be good enough, knowledgeable enough, or devoted enough to uphold the pristine traditions of the Renaissance era. They fervently believed that they were the only "true keepers of the genuine Renaissance way of life." They did agree on one thing. The club members agreed that they were angry with Harrison for suggesting the idea of hiring the consultants.

The club failed due to the economic strain. None of the members ever spoke to Harrison again. In true Renaissance fashion, he was "excommunicated" from the group and no longer permitted into their private Philosophers Cave.

STRATEGIES FOR SUCCESS:

The lessons of the past hold great value for the present, but they cannot be an exact blueprint for contemporary life. It is unrealistic, and economically unfeasible, for either individuals or businesses to attempt to live in the past, especially if it is a romanticized version of the Renaissance! As we venture outside the cave of beliefs masquerading as "facts," we grow. Discuss, test, and argue competing facts and ideas. Venture outside the cave of "this is how it has always been done" into "this is how it could now be done."

TIME MACHINE ACTIVITY:

The past is often an attractive location because historical outcomes are certain and therefore comfortably understood and analyzed from a distance. Imagine entering a time machine and give each participant three minutes to tell which historical era and location they would choose as their destination.

DISCUSSION IDEAS:

Would they like to experience a specific event? Meet a historical person? Would they like to have a one-way ticket and remain in the past, or just visit? Is the past better than the present? A fun group activity would be to watch and discuss the imaginative and entertaining time-travel Woody Allen movie *Midnight In Paris.* Discuss as a group how we can improve the present so that years from now it will be a past worth visiting!

FORTY SIX

POSITIVE PSYCHOLOGY

"What doesn't kill us makes us stronger" ~ Friedrich Nietzsche

During his Presidential speech at the American Psychological Association's 1998 convention, psychologist Martin Seligman urged his colleagues to focus less on mental distress, and more on positive strengths.

Seligman stated: "We believe that a psychology of positive human functioning will arise, which achieves a scientific understanding, and effective interventions, to build thriving individuals, families, and communities." He believed that positive psychology should "nurture genius and talent" and "make normal life more fulfilling."

Using the concepts of Positive Psychology, instead of diagnosing problems to be solved, individuals are encouraged by their mental health professionals to exhibit a positive life attitude. This positive life attitude creates an environment for increased success. Positive psychology studies show that people will indeed "rise to the occasion" when faced with adverse circumstances. The success rate is increased if the individual is given consistent encouragement.

EXAMPLE:

Jasmine was a follower. She had always been a follower. Being "in charge" required responsibility, and responsibility required giving orders. She liked being told what to do, then, if something wasn't correct, it wasn't her fault. She disliked having to think for herself. Following was comfortable and easy.

When her Supervisor was on vacation, Jasmine was called on to be in command because of her seniority. Her co-workers understood that Jasmine would make no decisions and issue no orders. Issues requiring managerial decision would have to wait until the Supervisor returned. Stepping into a position of authority made Jasmine feel nervous, but she rationalized that it wasn't really a potential problem. Emergency situations never occurred, and she wanted to receive the extra salary for being Substitute Supervisor "on duty."

While the "real" Supervisor was on vacation, an earthquake severely damaged the factory. There was fire, collapsed masonry, and general chaos. Communication networks failed. Jasmine couldn't contact management, or emergency services. She was without back-up, and was the "on duty" Supervisor. This was no fire drill; people needed her to lead them.

Jasmine wanted to run away but didn't. She had responsibilities. She started issuing emergency evacuation orders. To her own surprise, she found herself efficiently "rising to the occasion."

People were depending on her to take control of the situation. There was no one else to follow. Jasmine was forced to "take charge." If she had time to think, she would have been afraid to act. There was no time for negative personal reflection. There were no mental health professionals to analyze her weaknesses. She mustered positive psychology, took three deep breaths, and moved forward.

Jasmine remembered the mandatory fire drills, and the location of emergency medical equipment. She remained calm and focused. She delegated tasks efficiently and clearly. The injured were carried to safety, the fire was quenched, and everyone evacuated the area just before the ceiling collapsed.

Jasmine was in command. She was a heroine. When the emergency was over, she received a company promotion and substantial media attention. Jasmine was very proud of herself.

When things returned to normal, Jasmine remained proud of her accomplishments and more confident in her abilities, but she was delighted to let the "real" Supervisor resume the responsibility of day-to-day command.

STRATEGIES FOR SUCCESS:

Have you ever been forced to "rise to the occasion?" Perhaps not as dramatically as Jasmine, but we have all used positive psychology principles. Jasmine wasn't weak; she was complacent and afraid to risk "being blamed" for failing. When circumstances forced her to take the initiative, she summoned her inner strength and, using positive psychology, took successful control of the situation. Look for participant strength, rather than focusing on weakness. Everyone should be valued and encouraged to participate. Encourage innovative solutions. Place the focus on achieving a successful outcome going forward, instead of focusing on staving off the problems of the past.

POSITIVE VS NEGATIVE ACTIVITY:

Divide the participants into two groups. The first group will each have two minutes to describe an unrewarding work experience. After the first group has finished, the second group will each have two minutes to describe a rewarding one. (Note: You can also talk about personal experiences, but work experiences will have greater similarities for discussion.)

DISCUSSION IDEAS:

What are the similarities and differences between the stories? What could have been done to change the negative experiences into positive experiences? How did it feel to relate the stories? Did it recall the original emotions? Has the passage of time given new perspective to the negative experiences as well as the positive ones?

FORTY SEVEN

PRAGMATISM

"The ideal man bears the accidents of life with dignity and grace, making the best of circumstances." ~ Aristotle

Pragmatism is really the practical business of living. The only issues that matter are practical issues that make a difference to the outcome. Philosophical questions with no practical application are deemed useless. The problem is that we need to determine which issues are "useless," which creates the following pragmatic questions:

Who decides which issues are practical, and which are a waste of time? How is the decision made? How can we know which matters are practical issues that make a difference to the outcome, when the outcome has not been determined?

EXAMPLE:

Lucy owned a floral shop directly across from the busiest traffic intersection in town. Ordinarily, it was a prime retail location. The problem was that pedestrians were being injured crossing the intersection at an alarming rate. Within the last six months, two people had been killed, and eight struck by vehicles. Lucy couldn't sell flowers if customers were too frightened to cross the street.

The intersection had been there for years, but all of the accidents were recent. The pragmatic question was: "What caused the problem, and what could be done to prevent it from reoccurring?"

Everybody in the commercial area agreed that something needed to be done, but nobody could agree on exactly what that "something" was. Businesses were failing due to lack of revenue. Matters were made worse when the local newspaper published a front-page article indicating that the intersection was "cursed." Lucy was reluctant to volunteer, but the situation was going from bad to worse. She proposed a pragmatic plan for citizen action to correct the situation.

A group of concerned citizens, led by Lucy, the other merchants, and a pedestrian who had been injured, organized a citizen advocacy group. They carefully thought about the problem, and discussed how and when the incidents occurred. By analyzing the evidence, they quickly discerned a pattern.

The citizen group researched what had changed within the preceding six months. They discovered that the police department had shortened the traffic light pattern in an effort to increase traffic violation revenues.

The group, led by Lucy and the other merchants, agreed upon a course of action that included requesting re-scheduling of the traffic light sequencing. Their proposals were instituted. The intersection was no longer a pedestrian deathtrap, and business improved.

STRATEGIES FOR SUCCESS:

Pragmatism doesn't happen in a vacuum; we need to decide exactly what is the desired pragmatic, and workable, outcome. Lucy formed a committee to evaluate the problem and suggest a specific solution that was capable of immediate implementation. When dealing with multiple parties, deciding upon the issues, and their pragmatic solutions, is a group activity requiring research, discussion, thought, experimenting (or "beta testing") and agreed upon conclusions.

PRAGMATIC SOLUTION ACTIVITY:

Divide the group into a minimum of two teams each seated at a table. Give each team a thin plastic bowl filled to the brim with water. The bowl should be flimsy enough so that it is difficult to lift without squeezing the sides and losing some of the water. Disposable bowls are a perfect choice. Each team will pass the water bowl completely around the table. There are no rules concerning the method of passing or the speed. The team with the most water left in the bowl and the driest table wins.

DISCUSSION IDEAS:

Passing the bowl successfully is a simple problem, what pragmatic solution did each team devise? What did the winning team do and how did they decide on the winning strategy? What was the most imaginative solution? I once saw a team decide to empty the water into their used coffee cups, pass the bowl, and refill it — their bowl was full and the table was dry!

FORTY EIGHT

PRE-CONCEIVED NOTIONS

"The good news is that the moment you decide that what you know is more important than what you have been taught to believe, you will have shifted gears in your quest for abundance. Success comes from within, not from without." ~ Ralph Waldo Emerson

As an experiment to determine the validity of medical definitions distinguishing the "sane" from the "insane," David Rosenhan sent eight friends to hospital emergency rooms claiming to hear voices repeating the words "hollow," "empty" and "thud." This behavior fulfilled the minimum general requirements for a diagnosis of mental illness.

They were all diagnosed as schizophrenic, and admitted to psychiatric units. After admission, they promptly began to act normally, and reported that the voices had disappeared. The fake patients remained hospitalized, some for several weeks. Their normal behavior was repeatedly diagnosed as symptomatic of their purported illness.

The schizophrenia diagnosis was the pre-conceived notion used to interpret all thoughts and actions, leading to seemingly logical but actually erroneous conclusions.

EXAMPLE:

Nicholas thought that golf was a stupid game. He was absolutely certain that it was a ridiculous waste of time. While he had never actually played golf, he decided he was entitled to make this claim because he had watched golf tournaments on television. Players used a stick to hit a ball into a cup embedded in the ground. A chimpanzee could do it.

Nicholas was part of a corporate management team. To encourage team camaraderie, and cooperation, the team members were required to attend corporate "outings." The annual corporate "outing" was a luxurious five-day golfing retreat.

Nicholas didn't want to play golf for five days, but participation was mandatory. He was forced to rent golfing equipment, and prepare to play the game. He watched golf instruction videos and computer tutorials to gain a basic understanding of the rules, but he never physically practiced.

To his surprise, when Nicholas arrived at the golf course and started to actually play, the game was more difficult than it appeared to be. There was strategy, calculation, and specific sticks for specific purposes. Most interestingly, golf was a social pastime that encouraged networking opportunities both on and off the course. The golfing retreat was indeed a team building experience. After each professionally taught session, they discussed strategies, swings, wind calculations, and other golfing experiences with enthusiasm.

It was a team "bonding" experience, and it was fun. Nicholas decided to purchase his own set of clubs and invest in professional golf lessons, in preparation for the next corporate retreat.

STRATEGIES FOR SUCCESS:

We all have pre-conceived notions, and like Nicholas, we are certain that our notions are correct. Golf is "just a game," but his jaundiced preconceptions nearly prevented Nicholas from participating in a team bonding experience. Although we usually think of negative examples, preconceptions are often positive. They help us to anticipate, imagine, categorize and make sense of the world. The goal is to be aware of our own preconceived notions, and the preconceptions of others, and to be willing to accommodate change.

PEOPLE PRECONCEPTIONS ACTIVITY:

Divide the group into teams of six to eight participants. Give each team the same four photographs of different types of people. The photos should depict people of differing gender, age, ethnicity, clothing style, and overall appearance. Have the teams examine the photos and make judgments concerning the vocation, music preference, and shopping habits of the person depicted. Write down the judgments and present them to the entire group.

DISCUSSION IDEAS:

Are the judgments similar or dissimilar? Was there immediate consensus among the team members or substantial discussion concerning the results? Did we look at the same pictures and see different people? Why?

FORTY NINE

PREJUDICE

"A great many people think that they are thinking when they are merely rearranging their prejudices." ~ William James

Prejudice makes everything worse. There is a natural tendency to gravitate to people "like us," but we need to connect with "others" too. The best solution to prejudice is personal contact and inter-group experience.

Studies conducted in sectarian trouble spots, such as Northern Ireland, confirm that it's difficult to de-humanize a group of fellow humans when you actually know and like someone from the "other" group. To do this, the "other" must be viewed as a representative of their group, the contact must be reasonably sustained, and all parties must be treated with respect.

EXAMPLE:

Sophia hated vegetarians. She personally refused to eat green food, considering it the color of mold and decay. She had never actually met a vegetarian. All of her friends, family and acquaintances were enthusiastic carnivores.

Furthermore, Sophia's grandmother, who was a professional chef, considered vegetarians "difficult to cook for because they didn't eat what everybody else was eating." She taught Sophia that being a vegetarian was "unnatural."

It was an office tradition to celebrate team member birthdays with lunch at a restaurant chosen by the honoree. The honoree selected a highly recommended vegetarian restaurant. Sophia wanted to refuse her invitation, but the entire corporate management team was attending, and she wanted to network. She attempted to dissuade the honoree, but he was adamant about his restaurant selection. Sophia came prepared. She swallowed anti-nausea medication before arriving at the party, and chose the seat nearest to the restrooms…just in case she had to run.

To her amazement, the food was delicious, and most of the dishes were not green in color. The vegetarian proprietor was very nice, taking the time to explain the philosophy and the health benefits of a vegetarian lifestyle. Nobody seemed "unnatural." Her team members, and the honoree, were enthusiastic about the food. Sophia tasted everything, and she didn't even feel queasy. Everyone agreed that the party was a rousing success.

While Sophia did not become a vegetarian, she did change her mind about people who were.

STRATEGIES FOR SUCCESS:

Prejudice is an extreme form of preconceived notions. While preconceptions are usually acquired through personal experience, or at least personal opinion, prejudice is the internalization of a bias or belief taught by someone else. In the example above, a beloved and respected grandmother is used as the arbiter of right food and wrong food. In order to counteract prejudice, the contact needs to be sufficient to create a more positive attitude. Extended contact would, of course, be beneficial, but even casual experimenting will encourage common understanding and continued willingness to communicate.

FIELD EXPERIENCE ACTIVITY:

It's easy to talk about prejudice and righteously teach about tolerance and understanding in the abstract, but experience is the greatest teacher. Plan a volunteer day at the local Food Bank helping the clients select supplies, register for assistance, or some other volunteer capacity that encourages personal interaction between the volunteers and the beneficiaries.

DISCUSSION IDEAS:

Before going to the Food Bank, discuss the type of people the participants expect to encounter and write down the group opinions. Reconvene after the volunteer adventure and discuss whether or not the opinions have changed. Why?

FIFTY

PROSPECT THEORY

"Who is wise? He that learns from everyone. Who is powerful? He that governs his passions. Who is rich? He that is content. Who is that? Nobody." ~ Benjamin Franklin

Daniel Kahneman received the Nobel Prize in Economics for developing the Prospect Theory of "behavioral economics." Although the study itself involved risk taking when gambling, the underlying hypothesis seeks to understand how people actually behave, in defiance of supposedly rational behavior.

Psychologically, we think about the potential for loss differently than the potential for gain. According to Prospect Theory, "risk seeking for losses" people will gamble on a potential large loss to avoid a certain small loss. Those who prefer a small certain gain to gambling on a large uncertain gain are described as "risk adverse for gains."

EXAMPLE:

Isaac was Chairperson of the raffle committee for a local charity. He and his fellow committee members had worked hard to gather desirable prize donations. The prize offerings were splendid, but raffle ticket sales were sluggish. The charity fundraiser attracted prominent business people from all over the community. Attendance at the gala was a 500-dollar-per-person donation. Gala tickets were a sell-out. The raffle tickets were only five dollars each, and sales were slow.

Isaac and his committee didn't understand why their ticket sales were under-performing. In addition to the raffle tickets, the charity was also selling a large chocolate bar for a five-dollar donation. Chocolate sales were skyrocketing. Isaac contacted a friend who was an expert economist, and explained the situation. The economist theorized that although each raffle ticket was a chance to win a prize valued far in excess of the single ticket price, there was also a chance that the purchaser would lose their five-dollar investment. Potential purchasers were risk adverse, preferring to make a large donation to attend a party, or make a small donation to receive a candy bar. Raffle tickets were an uncertain payout.

The candy bar committee was winning, and Isaac hated to lose. He needed to describe purchasing raffle tickets as a positive opportunity for gain…much better than a candy bar! The raffle ticket committee developed a new sales strategy. Instead of emphasizing the risky nature of purchasing a prize "chance," they decided to emphasize the desirability and dollar value of the raffle items. They also limited the number of raffle tickets to be issued, so that definite odds-of-winning could be calculated and promoted.

Isaac created an online catalogue with prize photos and tantalizing descriptions. Prizes that had no definite monetary value (such as dinner with the Mayor) were listed as "priceless." The committee revised their marketing strategy. They offered five raffle tickets for twenty dollars…buy four, get one free. Ticket sales soared. The raffle committee was a huge success.

STRATEGIES FOR SUCCESS:

Psychological presentation is important. Isaac didn't alter the deal; he altered the manner of presentation to give it a more positive marketing slant. He turned a perceived undesirable into a perceived desirable. Prospect Theory also applies to negotiation tactics. Whether describing a gamble, a proposal, or a disputed issue, we can significantly alter the outcome by changing our description and "marketing" strategy. Consciously decide whether to negatively describe the situation as a chance of a loss, or a positive opportunity for a gain.

GOOD YEAR BAD YEAR ACTIVITY:

When remembering an event we can focus on the positive aspects and remember it favorably or focus on the negative aspects for an unfavorable result. Our perception depends upon internalized Prospect Theory interpretation. Pass a bowl filled with enough pennies for every participant to choose one. The penny issue years should vary and be less than fifteen years old. Ask the participants to divulge the year on their penny and tell the group something interesting that happened to them in that year.

DISCUSSION IDEAS:

Were most of the stories positive or negative? Can we remember the exact details or is the memory our interpretation of the facts? How did we choose which story to tell?

FIFTY ONE

PROXIMAL DEVELOPMENT ZONE

"A good example has twice the value of good advice." ~ Albert Schweitzer

In order to better understand how the human mind develops, Dr. Lev Vygotsky studied the learning process of small children. He determined that they developed learning primarily through interaction with "experts," their adult caretakers. During their formative years, children eventually "internalize" the problem solving process.

Vygotsky created the term "zone of proximal development" to describe the learning gap between the child's actual and potential intellectual development. This "zone of proximal development" research has also been applied to adults. We are constantly learning new ideas and expanding our potential. Throughout our lives, we acquire knowledge and new skills in collaboration with people who already possess them. This intellectual development is enhanced when the "expert" provides encouragement and instruction to create a "scaffold" within which the student can exercise their enhanced knowledge and create a successful solution.

EXAMPLE:

Chelsea liked being able to predict what was going to happen. She was comfortable with routine, and she disliked having her daily rituals disrupted. She also disliked independent thinking. She didn't welcome new ideas. The "way things had always been done" was the way she wanted to do them.

Chelsea worked on an assembly line building machines for a large corporation. Her job was repetitive, and she enjoyed it. Nothing ever changed. She had worked on the assembly line doing the same job, with the same fellow workers, for twenty years. They worked the same shift, ate together in the company lunchroom, and went home when the shift concluded. Their pay was union negotiated, and everyone was satisfied.

A multinational conglomerate purchased the company. The products were modernized, and so was the manner of production. Routine clerical jobs were outsourced to non-unionized labor in different countries. The assembly lines were completely automated.

Chelsea was downsized, and replaced by a robot. The robots replaced the entire assembly line crew. As part of their "redundancy" package, they received optional classes to "re-train" them for entry into the modern workforce.

They were afraid to learn new skills and get new jobs. What if they couldn't? What if they had already exceeded their "zone of proximal development?" They had no choice. They needed new paychecks. They had to try. The former assembly line crew decided to stay together and take the same re-training classes. They wanted to help each other learn the same new skills.

The classes emphasized practical, hands-on, skill training. It was a lot of work, and the students were exposed to many new ideas. Every day was different. There was no comfortable routine. They were forced to learn new computer skills, and new mechanical skills. They started the classes grudgingly, but it was so interesting that they began to enjoy going.

New "scaffolds," new ideas, were being created. Upon class completion, they graduated with highly marketable workplace skills, and impressive training credentials.

Chelsea and her friends were filled with new ideas, new "scaffolds," new entrepreneurial abilities, and new enthusiasm. Their "zones of proximal development" increased tenfold. They were proud, and determined to never again be "cogs in the corporate wheel."

They already understood how to build machinery. They had now been trained to analyze and understand business procedures. They had also learned how to market products successfully, and control production costs. Instead of applying for new jobs, they started a new business marketing a more cost-efficient, compact, and modern product. They went into direct competition with their former employer.

It was scary, but exciting. There were challenges. Every day was different. Nothing was routine. The business grew and was successful; no longer could they be replaced by robots.

STRATEGIES FOR SUCCESS:

Have you used the expression "outside my comfort zone" to describe a new situation? What you're really talking about is the imagined limits of your proximal development zone. The "limits" are "imagined" because just like Chelsea and her colleagues, the zone has infinite possibilities for expansion. In addition to academics, we all learn by observing and interacting with others. Leaning into a challenge can encourage new ideas, new solutions, and new skills. Learning not only makes the process more interesting, it creates the "scaffold" for a successful outcome.

SOMEONE ELSE ACTIVITY:

When we need to expand our proximal development zone as a group it is often easier to start by considering the options within the context of a hypothetical. Consider the issues from the imagined viewpoint of a celebrity or historical figure. More than one scenario can be explored to imagine various solutions and viewpoints. Celebrities are a fun choice especially when they have flamboyant personalities. Historical figures such as Abraham Lincoln and Mark Twain will encourage a more reasoned hypothetical solution.

DISCUSSION IDEAS:

Who should we choose for our hypothetical? How do we know what their viewpoint would be under these circumstances? Would our chosen example need to expand their proximal development zone to reach a solution? How can we apply the hypothetical discussion to reality?

FIFTY TWO

PSYCHOANALYSIS

"To enjoy the things we ought, and to hate the things we ought, has the greatest bearing on excellence of character." ~ Aristotle

Sigmund Freud famously developed Psychoanalysis as a behavioral theory. He theorized that many psychological difficulties were the result of sexual conflict. We are going to ignore the sexual parts (pun intended!) and concentrate on the behavioral manifestations.

As we discussed in Chapter 15, Freud proposed that everyone's personality has three parts: the "Id" which seeks immediate gratification; the "Ego" which makes rational decisions; and the "Superego" which makes moral judgments. According to Freud, these three forces within us are constantly creating personality conflicts including neurosis, repression, denial, guilt, anxiety, and meaningful dreams. Alfred Adler and Carl Jung later modified Freud's theories.

Jung disputed the personality structure concept, and rejected Freud's emphasis on sexual influence. Adler's more contemporary "social development theory" proposed that people are significantly motivated by self-preservation, social factors, and power.

EXAMPLE:

Martin had a huge "Id," a small amount of "Ego," and very little "Superego." Basically, he was immature and self-centered. He was motivated by self-preservation and the opinions of his peers on Facebook and Twitter. He lacked the "super ego" capacity to make moral judgments and discern proper behavior for himself. He had excellent real-life role models including his family members, teachers, and colleagues, but he was obsessed with celebrity opinions.

Martin spent hours online every day, "checking out" the latest trends. He didn't want to be a celebrity because he lacked the self-confidence to envision becoming famous. He just wanted to imitate whichever celebrity was currently popular.

Martin spent many work hours checking and posting on his Facebook page. His co-workers, many of whom shared his personality traits, were also enjoying social media during work hours. Their supervisor noticed that very little productive work was being done due to the amount of corporate time spent "Facebooking." Social media connections were banned from the workplace.

Martin and his friends were panic-stricken. How would they know what to do? How would they know what everyone else was doing? How would they know how to behave? They were banned from everything that mattered!

They considered quitting their jobs, but they liked being paid, and they couldn't find an employer who was more lenient concerning constant social networking. Bummer! Martin was forced to behave (at least during work hours) without constant outside affirmation. Once he started to recover from the shock, he discovered that he rather liked being more "socially developed."

Martin was forced to think for himself. He developed conflicting emotions, but he also developed new and interesting ideas. He decided to seek, and achieved, a workplace promotion to a more well-paid and responsible job. He more fully participated in teamwork, and volunteered for committees that now interested him. He was still motivated by the most recent trends, but they no longer controlled him. Martin was becoming a responsible adult.

STRATEGIES FOR SUCCESS:

Martin needed to mature into a responsible adult instead of a self-indulgent peer dependent teenager, regardless of his actual biological age. When dealing with an underdeveloped Ego coupled with an overdeveloped Id, recognize that unconscious motivating factors influence participant behavior. Adler's social factor modification of Freud's original theory is particularly useful. People are frequently motivated by self-preservation, self-affirmation, and power.

Think about the psychological ramifications of individual behavior and attitude. Once we understand the underlying motivations, we can negotiate successfully.

I HEAR YOU ACTIVITY:

Negotiation is an exercise in effective listening. Instead of listening carefully for speaker underlying meaning, we interpret and mentally process what was said by filtering the words through our own underlying unconscious motivation. Divide the group into partners and issue each pair identical index cards with two discussion questions.

The questions should involve non-controversial personal opinions such as favorite food, favorite vacation spot, or describe your dream job. The first partner will answer the first question by speaking about the subject non-stop for three minutes. The listeners cannot ask questions, they just listen. When the speaker finishes, the listener will have one minute to summarize what was said. The partner roles then reverse for the second question.

DISCUSSION IDEAS:

Was it difficult to speak non-stop for three minutes without listener interaction? How difficult was it to listen without asking questions? Were the summaries accurate and did they reflect the most important presentation points? Why not?

FIFTY THREE

PYGMALION EXPECTATIONS

"All the people like us are We. And everyone else is They." ~ Rudyard Kipling

In the George Bernard Shaw play *Pygmalion* (*My Fair Lady*), the flower girl, Eliza Doolittle, transforms into a society lady by learning to "act" in the proper manner. The transformation is more than physical appearance and speech patterns. The real transformation is her acceptance by established society members, and the effect this acceptance has upon her attitude and expectations, both positive and negative.

Expectations of peers, authority figures, and other influencers strongly shape personal opinions, attitude, ability to compromise, and behavior. Like Eliza, we learn to "act" in the proper manner — external mandates — to fulfill these internalized expectations. Problems occur when group participants have differing expectations and goals.

EXAMPLE:

Julie had just graduated with an MBA from a prestigious university. She had an impressive academic record, but no actual work experience. All of her professors (and her mother) agreed that she was a wonderful and gifted student with unlimited potential. She was a "star."

Julie expected to "shine" at her new job with a large corporation. She had always been the "best" at everything. Although she was hired for an entry-level position, that didn't bother Julie. She was certain that she would be project manager in six months, if not sooner.

What Julie didn't understand, but soon learned, was that all organizations have an internal "culture." A way of doing things that is already in place, and new individuals are expected to conform to the unwritten rules. Julie was arrogant to her co-workers. She was forced to switch departments, and take a reduction in pay. She learned to be polite.

Julie expected to dress like a student. Julie learned to observe her workplace surroundings, and the appearance of her co-workers. She purchased a conservative business suit. Still she saw herself as "the one who knows" and was known for being outspoken; and frequently wrong. She learned to value the experience and opinions of others.

She learned to listen, observe, and consider. Just like Eliza Doolittle, Julie learned.

STRATEGIES FOR SUCCESS:

One of the reasons *My Fair Lady*, and *Pygmalion* before it, are theater classics still popular today is because the new recruit fitting-in to the established culture is such a universal theme, especially in the workplace. The larger and more well-established the organization, the larger and more well-established the "culture." When forming a new group for a specific purpose, agree upon the specific goal and projected outcome as a "first step." Create a written mission statement, taking into consideration the existing organizational or social culture, and regularly review it individually and as a group. Measure progress, discuss expectations, and be aware of outside influences.

EXPECTATIONS ACTIVITY:

Group expectations are a powerful motivator for personal change. In *Pygmalion*, Eliza Doolittle is expected to follow her mentor's idea for evolving; conform to the existing social culture. When expectations are clearly defined, we tend to behave in accordance with the expectation, causing it to be realized. Ask the participants to relate a story where they surprised even themselves by meeting, and exceeding, expectations.

DISCUSSION IDEAS:

How were the expectations defined? Did you have a mentor? Have you ever mentored anyone, and what was the result? As a fun group activity, watch the movie *My Fair Lady* and discuss the implications of Eliza's transformation.

FIFTY FOUR

RADICAL DOUBT

"Man is a mystery. It needs to be unraveled, and if you spend your whole life unraveling it, don't say that you've wasted your time. I am studying that mystery because I want to be a human being." ~ Fyodor Dostoyevsky

When Rene Descartes decided to doubt the Jesuit teachings of his masters, he declared: "There was no such learning in the world as I had been led to hope." In his "Meditations on First Philosophy," Descartes created the theory of "radical doubt." He was searching for a single belief that was without doubt. The only belief that satisfied the "radical doubt" criteria was: *Cogito ergo sum* (Latin for "I am thinking, therefore, I exist").

We all have doubts; we are all human. But some people insist upon practicing the concept of "radical doubt" without discretion.

They require "proof" for everything, impeding progress. They want to constantly prove that they are thinking; therefore, they exist. They forget that they are not the only ones.

EXAMPLE:

Adrian was a tenured university professor of philosophy. He considered himself to be a philosopher, and he loved passionate debate. He enjoyed the challenge and satisfaction of winning an argument, even if the topic was unimportant. He argued that the "Socratic Method" demanded demonstrable proof of everything, even the fundamental fact of existence.

Adrian also enjoyed being the center-of-attention. It didn't bother him if the attention was negative. He greatly enjoyed being annoying; it was amusing. The university administrators knew that Adrian was a tenured professor, so his position was secure. He could not be fired, no matter how bombastic he became.

Adrian repeatedly interrupted meetings and class sessions to demand proof concerning the topic under discussion. He did not reasonably demand proof of relevant facts in dispute so that the truth could be ascertained. Adrian demanded proof of basic assumptions not in dispute. It was time consuming and counter-productive. His colleagues and students were very annoyed.

Students in the philosophy department refused to take his classes. Colleagues refused to include him in meetings. He was impossible to have a discussion with, because he constantly, and publicly, argued instead of answering a question. As his behavior grew increasingly offensive, the School Administrators knew something needed to be done.

The Dean of the University created a special research position for Adrian. It did not involve student classes, and he did not need to attend meetings. Adrian would study and research the philosophical meaning of existence from a cross-cultural perspective.

Adrian was delighted. He connected with other philosophers on an international level using the Internet. They argued constantly, testing theories, and discovering new and exciting avenues of enlightenment. Adrian established an International Society of Philosophers. Overtime this group acquired a worldwide reputation for philosophical excellence. He published books, wrote papers, and lectured to sold-out audiences. His reputation grew, and so did the prestige of his university.

Still, Adrian questioned everything, but not just to be annoying. He posed questions to force people to think. He initiated arguments to find workable conclusions. Adrian earned an international reputation as one of the world's greatest contemporary philosophers.

STRATEGIES FOR SUCCESS:

Adrian was assured of his position because of tenure, and he was bored. We have all encountered management level administrators who enjoy baiting the lower ranks because they seemingly have nothing better to do than play power games. Radical Doubt, although sometimes appropriate in complex situations, should not be employed as power tactic, positioning ploy, or a stalling device to prevent resolution. To create consensus all participants must agree, as a group, to accept certain basic principles, beliefs, and foundational facts as "true" and not requiring "proof." These foundational elements may seem like commonsense, but remember that commonsense is not very common.

IMPOSSIBLE TO PLEASE ACTIVITY:

This activity works best with a group of participants possessing higher education degrees — the more schooling they have, the more impossible teacher examples they've experienced! Allow each participant two minutes to tell their worst teacher horror story about the teacher who was impossible to please. For example, I had a law school professor who refused to give an "A" grade because "an "A" implies perfection and nobody is perfect!"

DISCUSSION IDEAS:

What made these educators so impossible to please? How did you handle the situation? Did the experience impact your communication and teaching style?

FIFTY FIVE

RESTRAINT BIAS

"Perform without fail what you resolve." ~ Benjamin Franklin

According to research conducted by psychologist Roy Baumeister, it is possible to become "ego-depleted" when forced to exhibit self-control. When we exercise a tremendous amount of willpower and restraint, we become exhausted and more likely to boomerang back to that thing we said we'd never do again.

The loss of control due to "Restraint Bias" occurs when we severely underestimate the intensity of our desires while experiencing a "hot state." We become "hot" when physical needs (hungry, exhausted, etc.) and emotional needs overpower our usual socially appropriate behavior. We lose restraint and succumb to temptation.

EXAMPLE:

Nora had a sarcastic sense of humor. Her personal friends and family members all thought that she was hysterically funny. She consciously restrained herself in the workplace because, as Department Supervisor, she felt compelled to set a good example. She understood that the workplace was a serious business environment and that sarcastic humor was inappropriate.

The company CEO had several repetitive behavior habits, and a rather pronounced facial tick — all symptoms of Tourette's syndrome, a neurological condition. He was also a micromanager, questioning the day-to-day decisions of all the supervisors, especially Nora. It was very annoying. Nora liked her job, but she didn't like her CEO. The constant supervision was intrusive. It impeded decision-making and delayed the production process. Nora complained to the company Founder, who was the father of the CEO.

A meeting was arranged to discuss the micro-management concerns. The company Founder refused to acknowledge the problem, and "sided" with his son. Nora was forced to concede. She was humiliated.

When Nora returned to her department, her team members asked for a synopsis of her meeting with upper management. Nora responded with an excellent, and hilarious, sarcastic imitation of the CEO defending his management style. Unfortunately, during her performance, the CEO entered the department on one of his daily inspections giving him the privilege of witnessing her mockery.

Nora was fired. The CEO is now micro-managing the new Department Supervisor, who is very careful to control his "restraint bias."

STRATEGIES FOR SUCCESS:

Remember the adage: "Practice makes perfect." Willpower takes practice, and needs practice to become second nature in social situations. Still, it's a workout to   continue to make a conscious decision to improve and control our knee-jerk impulses.

Whether we're parents, bosses, or employees, we set a good example by practicing restraint when tempted to respond in an inappropriate manner, and we should expect, and enforce, this standard equally.

Nora found it difficult to control her theatrical sense of humor. On the job, she worked to practice restraint, but a single witnessed incident proved fatal. She not only lost her position, she ruined her professional reputation. Loss of civility, and succumbing to "restraint bias," is always unacceptable.

EXPLODING ANGER ACTIVITY:

Everyone has been "angry enough to explode" at some point in their lives, especially when the anger was necessarily restrained. This activity is a visual representation of the explosion using a child's balloon and a balloon inflation hand pump. Stand in the front of the group and have participants call out annoyances, frustrations, and things that really make them angry. For every response, pump air into the balloon until we exhaust our grievances and the balloon bursts. If the balloon bursts quickly before we're finished, use an additional balloon. If the balloon refuses to explode, use a thumbtack.

DISCUSSION IDEAS:

How did it feel when the balloon finally burst? Was it surprisingly cathartic to voice these peeves? Did the participants agree on common frustrations, annoyances and anger issues?

FIFTY SIX

SCIENTIFIC REVOLUTIONS

"The only man who never makes mistakes is the man who never does anything."
~ Theodore Roosevelt

Thomas Kuhn determined that "normal science" takes place within a structure of paradigms — examples, models, and patterns — that form the rules and standards for any given scientific discipline. "Normal" was defined as within the foundations of accepted scientific knowledge.

"Scientific revolutions" are created when the prior paradigms are confronted with new information making them unworkable and creating crisis. New paradigms must be developed to end the crisis and move forward.

Analogous to "scientific revolutions," new information, new expert opinions, and new alliances create new foundational ideas that may create a crisis requiring resolution before the group can proceed. When foundational premises become unworkable, individual participants must embrace a new conceptual "normal" as a group.

Issues, ideas, and group goals have "revolutions" changing the structural paradigm. We may need to change direction, reconsider our goals, or modify our expectations.

EXAMPLE:

The new video game just wasn't selling, and Tobias didn't know why. He headed the Imagine Gaming company product management team, and everyone had agreed that the product was a great idea. The team had assumed that consumers would love it. The profit margins, and sales projections, were expected to be extraordinary.

They had launched the product in upscale markets appealing primarily to teenagers. It was inexpensive compared to their competitors' similar models, and it functioned flawlessly.

Tobias and his team were unpleasantly surprised. The product was perfect, except for the fact that it just wasn't selling. The reviewers didn't like it either, although they didn't give specific reasons. Tobias and his team debated what "not rad enough" meant. They didn't know. They had no choice. The product seemed great, but it obviously wasn't.

The product management team re-thought the entire concept. They realized that they did not understand how to successfully target the product's consumer demographic. They decided to seek expert advice.

Tobias fired the product-marketing firm, and hired a firm with proven success for reaching the teenage consumer target demographic. They brought in small focus groups of teenagers across the country to give their honest opinions. Side-by-side comparisons were done with competitor products. Every inch was examined, tested, and questioned.

Most importantly, Tobias and his team listened. They carefully analyzed the data, and reached consensus. They gained new understanding, and created new foundational premises. The individuals, as a group, embraced "revolution" and accepted a new "normal." The product packaging was re-designed. The functionality was upgraded. The shape was modified. Celebrity endorsements were procured.

The improved version was marketed as an entirely new product. Teenagers loved it. Reviewers loved it. Stores couldn't keep it in stock. It was "rad."

STRATEGIES FOR SUCCESS:

The reason Tobias and his team succeeded was because they carefully listened without preconception bias. They understood the necessity of becoming flexible and willing to embrace new knowledge. Realistic expectations change with the circumstances, and "revolution" should be welcomed as part of the "new normal" process.

EXPECTATION ACTIVITY:

Whenever groups participate in team activities, the participants have an expectation of equal treatment. Past activities have always provided everyone with equal materials and an equal opportunity to participate. But circumstances change and we can create a "new normal." Divide the group into teams of three and issue each team two one-dollar bills. Allow five minutes for the team members to negotiate who will keep the money.

DISCUSSION IDEAS:

How did the team decide who keeps the money? What did the participants who were given the funds promise to do in return for the money? Did one participant negotiate to keep the money, or was it divided between two people? Was the team member who received no funds satisfied with the result? Were there teams who couldn't decide? Why?

FIFTY SEVEN

SELF STEREOTYPE

"To be thrown upon one's own resources is to be cast into the very lap of fortune, for our faculties then undergo a development and display an energy of which they were previously unsusceptible." ~ Benjamin Franklin

This isn't the unreasonable stereotype used to judge someone else on the basis of physical or ethnic attributes. Self-stereotype is even more insidious.

Self-stereotype is a generalized, life-changing notion that we have internalized about ourselves. There are many examples of these strongly internalized biases. For instance: *Girls don't understand math. Boys can't cook. Women are empathetic. Men are rational.* These are all internalized self-stereotypes created by perceived cultural norms. Like all stereotypes, they are usually inherently wrong.

Researchers Claude Steele and Joshua Aronson referred to this social phenomenon as "stereotype threat." Stereotype threat has been documented in "intelligence tests." During experimental testing, female chess players played below their usual skill level when told that their opponent was male. Schizophrenia patients have also been observed to behave in a self-stereotypical manner after being told that the person they are interacting with knows of their diagnosis.

EXAMPLE:

Anna couldn't use a computer. She was the CEO of her company, and CEO's didn't need computer skills. That's why she had staff. Anna was 61 years old and she was convinced that people over sixty couldn't learn complicated new skills. She knew that this self-stereotype was the truth because she had read scientific research studies indicating that human brain cells start to die after the age of sixty.

In reality, Anna was afraid and embarrassed to even try. She didn't want to admit to her staff that she didn't know how, and she was afraid she might not be able to learn. She was the CEO. Therefore, she must know everything. She could not afford to show any vulnerability. She dreaded being perceived as incompetent.

Anna's company was active in multi-national markets. The corporate management team was constantly expanding their marketing efforts into major cities in different parts of the world. To facilitate corporate expansion, Anna needed to travel to an area where she would not have an English-speaking support staff. Technology assistance would be minimal. She was informed that communications with the United States office would be accomplished using the Internet and Skype conference calls.

Anna felt panic. She knew that she couldn't use the computer. She couldn't Skype. She couldn't even "turn the thing on." But most of all, she couldn't admit that she couldn't!

Anna hired a tutor. Not someone in her company. The tutor was an outsider who came to her home for private one-on-one lessons. Anna took a week of vacation days to concentrate. The tutor came for eight hours a day. Anna learned. She practiced the skills she would need. She took notes. She practiced some more.

Anna could use a computer. She could communicate anywhere in the world. She could Skype. She was ready. Anna was not afraid.

STRATEGIES FOR SUCCESS:

The fear of showing "weakness" is a common professional self-stereotype. We are afraid to be perceived as inadequate by our colleagues and superiors. Was Anna weak? Of course not, she was just inexperienced in technology and needed to learn a new skill set. When forced, Anna overcame her fear and self-stereotype of inadequacy, proactively hiring an expert instructor to remedy the situation.

Think about it. We all "know" certain generalizations about others and ourselves. Are they actually true? Do we act as though they are? The solution is personal acknowledgment of the danger of self-stereotype. The solution is personal acknowledgment of the danger of using stereotypes to influence our opinions of other people. The solution is constant vigilance.

SELF IMAGE ACTIVITY:

It's not how we actually look; it's how we perceive our appearance looks in the eyes of others that's important to self-image and self stereotyping. Give everyone a piece of drawing paper and a soft-tipped pen. Allow fifteen minutes to draw a self-portrait. Explain that sophisticated artistic ability is irrelevant; we are portraying our essence. Display the finished portraits side-by-side for group appreciation.

DISCUSSION IDEAS:

Looking at the exhibit, can we guess who each portrait represents? Once we have finished identifying the portraits, have each participant explain the details of their artwork. What do they have in common?

FIFTY EIGHT

SMALL WORLD

"Do not waste time bothering whether you "love" your neighbor; act as if you did. As soon as we do this we find one of the great secrets. When you are behaving as if you loved someone, you will presently come to love him. If you injure someone you dislike, you will find yourself disliking him more. If you do him a good turn, you will find yourself disliking him less." ~ C.S. Lewis

We have all been in situations where we meet a total stranger and discover that we have something or someone in common, and someone invariably says in surprise: "It's a small world!" Indeed it is, and this inter-connection between seemingly dissimilar people is the key to the scientific discipline of "small-world theory."

Sounds obvious? Studies indicate that everyone can be linked to everyone else in the world by as few as six intermediaries, which means that we all exist in a network of inter-connected units.

According to the scientific studies, these "units" are not necessarily other people. They are everything from friends and neighbors, to computers and multi-national companies.

EXAMPLE:

Thomas did not like his relatives, and he didn't encourage friendships. If he had known about the "small world theory," he would have been appalled. The thought that he might have connections within "six degrees of separation" to everyone else was not pleasant. He simply didn't want to know.

Thomas was forced to participate in a management team at work. He was competent and polite to fellow team members, but he didn't socialize. He had no interest in his team-mates outside of workplace issues.

Corporate management, in an effort to build team relationships, required all management level employees to attend a two-day "teambuilding workshop." Thomas thought that it was a ridiculous waste of corporate resources. But there he was, at a mandatory workplace compliance seminar, participating in a mandatory networking exercise. There was no way out, so he was grudgingly participating.

The networking exercise involved choosing a partner and asking a series of questions written on small cards provided by the networking facilitator. After five minutes of questions and answers, everyone changed partners. The exercise continued until everyone in the group had exchanged information with everyone else. Surprisingly, it was getting interesting. Thomas began learning about all sorts of common interests, common acquaintances, and common experiences.

Thomas discovered that the co-worker two offices down the hall, the one he'd never interacted with, and actually didn't remember, had attended grammar school with him. They decided to get together for beers after the seminar, and other participants decided to join them. After several beers, Thomas actually uttered the phrase "it's a small world."

STRATEGIES FOR SUCCESS:

As successful people and social creatures we live in groups both personally and professionally. As Thomas discovered, this is not a problem, interacting with others is a wonderful benefit of being human. When confronted with membership in a group of strangers, get to know each other as people. Create a convivial atmosphere for group participation. The group facilitator should encourage frequent time-outs for food and networking breaks so that everyone can discover their "six degrees" of inter-connections.

COLORFUL MEETING ACTIVITY:

We can't explore our interconnectedness if we don't meet each other and discover the "six degrees." Provide two large boxes of multi-colored crayons. Each participant gets to choose one crayon and then go around the room to find a partner with a similar color. Allow two minutes for the partners to discover similarities. After the first two minutes, have the participants partner up with someone holding a dissimilar crayon color. Allow two minutes to discover ways in which they are different from each other.

DISCUSSION IDEAS:

What was the most interesting thing that you learned? Was it easier to discover the similarities? Was two minutes enough time or will you continue the discussion during our next break?

FIFTY NINE

SOCIAL CONTRACT

"People who lean on logic and philosophy and rational exposition end by starving the best part of the mind." ~William Butler Yeats

The philosophical theory of Social Contract provides foundation for civil relationships with our fellow humans. We are all parties to the contract. There are two primary social contract theories. Thomas Hobbes argued that all humans are naturally violent and depraved. Hobbes thought that humans required a "social contract" with an absolute authority to prevent chaos.

Jean Jacques Rousseau argued that humans are "noble savages" who become corrupted by the inequality of civilized society. Rousseau thought that the "general will of the population" should be the social contract governing authority.

EXAMPLE:

Nobody was in charge. Lisa hated that! The employee focus group wasn't really a group. They were just a bunch of dissimilar people with a basic idea that something needed to be done. There was only one absolute certainty. Everyone was certain that the company was on the verge of bankruptcy due to mismanagement. They were all going to lose their jobs.

Lisa did not particularly like her job. The company was just as disorganized as the focus group, and it was nearly impossible to finish projects because of managerial indecision. However, she did like her steady paycheck.

Lisa was reluctant to volunteer. She knew that volunteers did not get paid, and they often got blamed if things went wrong. Lisa carefully analyzed her employment options. She was the supervisor of her department, she didn't want to go hunting for a new job, and no one else was coming forward to lead. Lisa volunteered to take control of the situation. She established rules of decorum, so that everyone could have a chance to be heard without interruption. In order to enforce the rules of decorum, she also established time limits for each speaker so that everyone would have an equal amount of attention.

Everyone had a suggestion, opinion, or recommendation for saving the company from bankruptcy. Carefully selected employee-based committees seriously considered all of the opinions, suggestions and recommendations.

Lisa established a regular committee-meeting schedule. She insisted that management participate equally, so that everyone could see that progress was being made. The combined committees established a timeline for financial stability. They looked at the company financial situation, and brought in financial planning experts to establish a workable budget. Marketing experts were brought in to create a plan for attracting new business. The "general will of the population" became the governing body of the company through committee involvement. They planned, organized, and kept the revitalization process focused.

Most importantly, everyone was included in the process. Everyone felt invigorated. They were working together as a team. They were invested in promoting and creating corporate success. They were all participants in the social contract and needed to preserve their jobs. The company did not go bankrupt. Lisa did not lose her paycheck. In fact, her paycheck increased substantially when she was promoted to a management position.

STRATEGIES FOR SUCCESS:

Teamwork is the foundation of success. Lisa's colleagues understood that if they didn't take action they were all going to fail, but they didn't understand the practical implementation required for a successful transition from idea to plan. Plans need facilitation and an organized leader with the clear vision to lead the group and take action.

Whichever social contract theory you prefer, the practical application is the necessity for clearly defined rules, equally enforced, to keep the process civil and moving forward. In addition to having clearly defined rules of behavior and procedure, there should also be a clearly defined method of appeal and a procedure for rule modification to prevent injustice.

TEAM BUILDING ACTIVITY:

The Social Contract depends upon trust. Team building and strong leadership is required in order to facilitate a successful outcome. Divide the group into teams and provide each team with a large piece of drawing paper and felt tip pens. Allow twenty minutes for each team to graphically depict the characteristics of a successful team and a strong group dynamic. Reconvene the entire group and compare depictions.

DISCUSSION IDEAS:

Were some teams more successful in reaching consensus? Why? Did all the teams depict overlapping characteristics? Define and discuss the results. Does this group embody the elements of a successful team and strong group dynamic? Why? If not, what can be done to improve the situation?

SIXTY

SOCIAL IDENTITY THEORY

*"When a hundred men stand together, each of them
loses his mind and gets another one."*
~ Friedrich Nietzsche

People love being part of a group. Human beings are inherently social animals, and we desire interaction with other humans. Professionals, and college students, join fraternal groups. People with a common interest form all types of groups. Everyone is born into, or deliberately decides to join, a cultural group. People form groups just to be members of a group. Nietzsche calls this propensity to belong or be part of a group "the herd mentality." This pack instinct can be dangerous when a leader is corrupt as we see in the example of Hitler enrolling the German people into the ranks of the Nazi Party or the American example of "The People's Temple" leader Jim Jones enlisting 900 people to die for the cause of their redemption. When misdirected, people in groups can be led to participate in their own destruction.

Groups require leaders. Psychologist Michael Hogg determined that group leaders are not chosen because they are "the best and the brightest." According to Hogg, group members choose the most "average" person as leader. They choose as their leader the person with whom they can most easily identify. The chosen leader must then prove his/her leadership ability by enhancing group stature and membership exclusivity.

When leaders connect with constituents or their team, they build both loyalty and personal integrity. The Leader's objective is to encourage enthusiasm and promote membership connection. If properly led, people will show unwavering allegiance to their chosen group, rationalizing their membership even if the group digresses from the original purpose.

Leaders seek to retain their position by reinforcing the group social identity. Unfortunately, history repeatedly shows us that leaders often maintain control through negative and often violent enforcement of social identity theory. Nazi Germany is a contemporary example of unsavory, but highly effective, political strategies supporting exclusivity, such as racism and stereotyping.

EXAMPLE:

Max loved college. It was his first experience living away from home. He had plenty of money, provided by his parents, so he didn't need a job. He could devote himself entirely to the pleasures of the college experience.

Max was invited to become a member of the most prestigious fraternity on campus. The fraternity was fantastic. Max was elected by the members to be the fraternity leader, and he knew exactly what everyone wanted. They partied continuously. Max made certain that all of the college girls wanted to party with all of the fraternity members.

Studying was non-existent and irrelevant because the fraternity had copies of the homework assignments. Fraternity members could just submit a pre-written assignment and receive a good grade.

Max very fondly remembered his college days. The fraternity members had been of "one mind." They wanted the same things, had the same goals, and enjoyed the same lack of responsibility. Max regarded his time in the fraternity as the happiest years of his life.

Even though it was two decades in the past, Max was still loyal to his fraternity "brothers." They no longer led similar lives, but they had kept in contact. Max worked in the Human Resources Department of a multinational corporation. When two of his "brothers" needed jobs, Max made certain that they received interviews, and were the successful candidates for positions in his corporation.

Past experiences as "brothers," along with new experiences as colleagues in the workplace, brought them even closer together. When they were all appointed to an employee relations committee, they were delighted. The three of them would really make a difference! The Committee Chairperson, who worked in a different division, immediately noticed that the three of them formed a clique. Everybody noticed.

They whispered and laughed with each other during committee meetings. When asked to participate in committee proceedings, the three "brothers" always espoused the exact same opinion. They were obviously exclusionary toward the other committee participants. They had formed a private group, just like their fraternity days, and Max was their leader just as he was President in their fraternity.

The Committee Chairperson was not pleased. She assigned them different tasks with different people. She re-arranged the seating so that they did not sit together. She created teams, assigning them carefully. She created an inclusive group dynamic, and did not permit small exclusionary sub-groups. At first, Max and his friends resented being separated, but they had no choice. The Committee Chairperson was in control, and her requirements were non-negotiable.

The "brothers" were forced to adjust to the new group dynamic. They developed new group connections, and successfully integrated into the group as workplace team members. The Committee Chairperson was now their group leader.

STRATEGIES FOR SUCCESS:

Max and his friends formed a clique to reinforce their shared social identity and cover up their inexperience. They were not men of integrity in the fraternity 20 years before nor were they used to working hard instead of taking shortcuts to appear successful. This bond between friends is socially appropriate in private, but highly disruptive in the workplace. The Committee Chairperson in our example was cognizant of good group dynamics and took appropriate steps to assert leadership and control.

Whenever we are the group leader, we need to be aware of sub-groups who speak-with-one-voice, especially if they have a strong leader who is attempting to exert control over the larger group. Michael Hogg is correct; leaders tend to be the most prototypical group members. They understand their followers and are able to manipulate them.

As a negotiation tactic, offering public respect and deference to the group leaders will acknowledge their position, and work to make compromise possible. As a workplace tactic, committee and sub-committee assignments can be used to manipulate the group dynamic by creating working relationships across group boundaries.

GROUP INSTINCT ACTIVITY:

Divide the group into teams and give each team a different picture of animals in an instinctively formed group. For example: a pride of lions, a herd of elephants, etc. Allow five minutes to discuss the reasons that these groups form in nature. Have each team present their reasoning to the entire group.

DISCUSSION IDEAS:

Do the same reasons for aggregating apply to human groups? What additional reasons do we have for joining groups? Is social identity always a conscious choice? Does participation in this group provide a temporary social identity?

SIXTY ONE

SOCRATES

"We can know only that we know nothing. And that is the highest degree of human wisdom." ~ Leo Tolstoy, *War and Peace*

Whether we were philosophy majors or not, we have all practiced the "Socratic Method" in school where we learned to ask pertinent questions that elicited reasoned answers from the teachers. We learned the same method from our parents and respected role models.

The "Socratic Method" requires asking, testing, and reasoning to seek the truth, even if the "truth" proves your foundational premise wrong. Socrates was deemed the "wisest man in Athens" because he knew that he knew nothing in an absolute sense. He knew only to ask questions and seek true answers.

EXAMPLE:

Katherine had a curious mind. She loved learning new ideas, and was always interested in "how things work." She asked lots of questions. The company computer systems needed modernization. The firm hired an outside IT consultant to create the software upgrade and install new hardware.

As the corporate managing partner Katherine was no IT expert, but she was fascinated by the proposed plans. She asked lots of detailed questions concerning the practical, everyday use of the upgrades, and their potential economic impact on the company.

By carefully listening to the answers, and constantly asking relevant follow-up questions, Katherine discovered that the IT consultants didn't understand the needs of her company. They were also charging for a custom designed system, but the planned installation was generic.

In addition to an entire list of technical problems, the network capacity was inadequate, security was practically non-existent, and day-to-day record keeping was going to be impossibly complicated. The recommended system was completely inadequate.

The IT consultant firm was fired. The company hired new experts who installed the appropriate system. A substantial amount of funds, and human resources, were saved. Katherine was rewarded with a promotion to CFO.

STRATEGIES FOR SUCCESS:

It is impossible to know everything; therefore we need to ask for instructions and explanations when we feel confused. Discourse is the key. Katherine didn't need to be a technology expert. She asked questions, and demanded reasoned answers. If she was unsatisfied with the answers, she asked for additional details until she understood the issues clearly. Careful reasoning, and analysis of alternative strategies, will create a clear plan of action.

ADVICE ACTIVITY:

Sometimes we refuse to ask for instructions and explanations because we are embarrassed to appear ignorant. Each participant writes a problem, concern, or question on the top of a sheet of paper. The papers are then passed to the person on the right who then has two minutes to write an answer, advice, or words of encouragement. All of the papers are circulated every two minutes to the next person on the right until everyone has had a chance to reply, and participants receive their original sheets back. Allow the entire group two minutes to read the responses that they received.

DISCUSSION IDEAS:

Is the advice useful? Are the problem solutions practical? Are you surprised by the results? Why?

SIXTY TWO

THEORY OF RELATIVITY

*"It isn't so astonishing, the number of things that I can remember,
as the number of things I can remember that aren't so."* ~ Mark Twain

Einstein's Theory of Relativity describes the interaction of matter, energy, space, and time. It is actually two theories. The theory of "Special Relativity" determined that nothing travels faster than the speed of light. This creates a groundbreaking scientific equation for the conversion of matter into energy, and energy into matter. The second theory, "General Relativity" postulates "space-time." This portion of the equation is extremely popular with science fiction writers, and serious scientists, because it proposes that time is a dimension with gravitational fields.

Why are we discussing the Theory of Relativity in such a simplistic and an unscientific manner? General Relativity theorizes the possibility of going back in time to change the present. Group participants, adverse parties, and human beings in general, often act as though time travel is not only present-day possible, they have actually done it!

Past events change in their minds, creating new unwarranted interpretations. Uncontroverted facts change, as though time travelers have altered the past for a better present.

EXAMPLE:

Adam was the recently hired Human Resources Manager for an international corporation. Because the corporation employed thousands of people in a multitude of job descriptions, there were always available positions. The Human Resources office received hundreds of job applications for each advertised opening. Every applicant was required to complete a preliminary, standardized, form listing basic qualifications and pertinent information.

The employment form was very straightforward. Each applicant was asked to provide relevant information including educational credentials and past employment experience. Before accepting the Human Resources job, Adam had always assumed that people were generally honest, and that they wouldn't lie about actual facts of their training. He was wrong.

Human Resources staff members checked basic factual assertions before the applications were sent to the proper department managers for interview consideration. More than fifty percent of the submitted applications failed this basic review. Another thirty percent of the applicants, who were granted personal interviews, were determined to have imaginatively embellished their credentials and past experience. It was the General Theory of Relativity. The past had been revisited, and improved. A substantial amount of valuable time had been wasted. Qualified people had not been hired. Something had to be done.

Adam decided to streamline the process. The standardized job application form was expanded. Proof of educational credentials was required to be attached at the time of submission. Every applicant was required to sign an affidavit attesting to the truth of the provided information. Prior employment references were required, and contacted.

The process wasn't perfect. There was still a certain amount of imaginative interpretation, but the most egregious falsifications were easily detected.

STRATEGIES FOR SUCCESS:

Adam created a practical solution to a common workplace problem. He also instituted a protocol that was replicable throughout the company and standardized for departmental use. Whenever confronted with assertions of prior conduct and factual representations, we should assume that time travel has not occurred, and gather factual proof. Remember that although "truth" is often a matter of perspective, and "proof" may be subject to interpretation, factual evidence always creates the foundation.

DETAILED MEMORY ACTIVITY:

For one minute, show the group a simple line drawing with a moderate amount of detail. I use a large coloring book picture of a barn with windows, a sun, clouds, trees and a fence. After the 60-second display, distribute paper and felt tip pens instructing the participants to duplicate the picture details. Allow five minutes for completion and compare results.

DISCUSSION IDEAS:

Was there a large variation in the number of details remembered? Were some details remembered but misplaced on the page? Did everyone believe that they were creating a factual representation of the original drawing?

SIXTY THREE

UTILITARIANISM

"Style, personality — deliberately adopted and therefore a mask — is the only escape from the hot-faced bargainers and money-changers." ~ William Butler Yeats

When creating the idea of Utilitarianism, John Stuart Mills postulated that an action is right if it promotes aggregate happiness (the greatest happiness for the most people). An action is wrong to the extent that it causes unhappiness or pain. Mills also defined happiness by degree of desirability, writing that: "No intelligent human being would consent to be a fool…even though they should be persuaded that the fool, the dunce, or the rascal is better satisfied with their lot than they are with theirs." Utilitarianism sounds good. The problem is its practical implications.

Public hangings make crowds happy therefore we could argue that hangings fulfill the utilitarian concept of "aggregate happiness." But would this interpretation be acceptable? The original philosophical concept has also been twisted into "the ends justify the means" type behavior.

"The ends justify the means" is a term originally associated with the utilitarian ideas of Niccolo Machiavelli (1469-1527) who believed that public and private morality should be defined as two separate concepts in order to rule effectively. As a result, a ruler must be willing to act immorally and resort to the methodical exercise of excessive force and deceit. Repressive governments, and totalitarian dictators all over the world, are ardent followers of Machiavellian utilitarianism.

EXAMPLE:

Vivien was economic results-oriented. She was highly successful in business, and proud of her economic standing and her social position. People of importance desired her acquaintance.

Vivien wasn't too fussy about her moral obligations. In fact, she didn't consider that she had any moral obligations. Moral codes of conduct did not apply to her. Vivien was the CEO of a multi-national investment firm, not the director of a bleeding heart charity. Charities needed moral codes. Successful companies couldn't afford morals; they needed to make money.

Vivien felt that she was above the law. Most laws and regulations were written by elected officials determined to market themselves as high-minded observers of ethical standards. Moral correctness appealed to voters, and voters elected the rule makers.

The laws were for the common public, and Vivien was not common. Whatever she needed, whatever she desired, she acquired it in the most efficient and utilitarian manner possible. She didn't need public votes, but she did need to satisfy the corporate share-holders. Shareholders were primarily interested in investment dividends. Her shareholders were extremely satisfied.

Vivien didn't waste time with political correctness, nor did she waste money with legal compliance. She was the CEO, and she managed her Board of Directors, and the management teams, like a dictatorship. Obedience was mandatory. Differing opinions recommending legal compliance were not only ignored, they were cause for termination. Vivien fired corporate employees and attorneys on a regular basis. Agreement with Vivien was required for continued employment. She believed that the ends always justify the means. The SEC regulations were merely moralistic suggestions.

In order to maximize investment dividends for her largest corporate clients, Vivien created an illegal "pyramid scheme." Small investors would lose their money, but the most important investors would become even wealthier. Most importantly, Vivien would be rich. When the "pyramid" collapsed, she planned to leave the country with her millions. Albeit corrupt, it was a fantastic utilitarian scheme. There would be aggregate happiness amongst the winning shareholders. Her only fiduciary duty was to herself. She was powerful. She got results.

Regulatory agencies, and the officials charged with enforcing the laws equally regardless of personal importance, were not impressed. They made gathering evidence against Vivien, and her associates, a law enforcement priority. Vivien was not as important in jail.

STRATEGIES FOR SUCCESS:

When the process is time-consuming, expensive, and tedious, it's easy to look for an expedient utilitarian solution to "get the job done" and declare successful completion. Utilitarianism is a practical, workable concept, but it should provide more than a "quick fix" for an underlying problem. Don't capitulate and permit a fundamental defect in the process that will cause the outcome to be questioned, and ultimately invalidated.

Vivien did more than compromise an ethical principle; she deliberately violated the law for her own economic benefit. If the laws are unreasonable, work to change them, but legal compliance cannot be ignored, manipulated or bullied. Seemingly utilitarian "short-cuts" may make everyone happy for the moment, but the foundation must be strong to prevent future unhappiness.

AESOP'S FABLES ACTIVITY:

Aesop's Fables have been preserved through the ages as morals tales because they are perfect examples of utilitarianism vs. ethical behavior. Either read out loud or distribute copies of "The Wolf and the Lamb," Aesop's famous tale of injustice in which a victim is falsely accused and killed despite a reasonable defense.

DISCUSSION IDEAS:

What is the purpose of the accusations, and what do they accomplish? Is the Aesop's wolf employing a utilitarian "shortcut" and reaching a Machiavellian conclusion? What should have been done? How does this fable relate to human behavior, and are there contemporary examples?

CONCLUSION

My favorite tale of transformation is *How the Grinch Stole Christmas* by Dr. Seuss. Why? The Grinch rejects his pre-conceived notions when presented with contradictory evidence, transforms through cross-cultural contact, and "carves the roast beast" as a gesture of goodwill.

In the beginning, the Grinch has had no personal contact with the Whos down in Whoville. He has watched them from a distance and drawn his own erroneous conclusions about their sentimental rituals. The Grinch doesn't know much about the Whos, but he knows that he hates them.

He hates them because they have warmer houses, better food, and a happy smugness in the comfort of their little town. Everything is right with them, and wrong with him.

Instead of attempting to improve his unpleasant situation, the Grinch decides to make the Whos as unhappy as he is. The Grinch steals the Whos' stuff. Why? Because the Grinch has developed a pre-conceived notion that stealing the Whos' stuff will please him by ruining their celebration and upending their happy lives.

This idea has been re-enforced by seemingly logical deductive reasoning. The Grinch has observed the townspeople delightedly preparing gifts and the feast. He draws a conclusion, based upon the fundamentally flawed premise of his prejudiced interpretation of the observed Who behavior, that their primary purpose is acquisition. When his plan doesn't work, the Grinch is shocked, confused, dismayed, and ultimately…after a three-hour "think"…transformed.

Dr. Seuss says that the Grinch's heart "grew three sizes that day." His mind grew, too. His understanding, his tolerance, and his willingness to see the Whos as individuals, all grew. We too can learn to understand, acknowledge, and respect diverse personalities and opinions. When we are willing see everyone as an individual, we can successfully get along with anyone.

How to Get Along With Anyone: 63 Strategies For Success is a journey into the minds of many diverse personalities, and an activity adventure in team building. I hope that you have enjoyed the journey, learned from the examples, and tried the activities. Thank you for traveling with me.

ADDITIONAL RESOURCES

Baron, Jonathan, *Thinking and Deciding* (2000)

Bazerman, Max, *Judgment in Managerial Decision Making* (1998)

Bazerman, Max and Ann Tenbrunel, *Blind Spots: Why We Fail to Do What's Right and What to Do About It* (2011)

Beilock, Sian, *Choke: What The Secrets of the Brain Reveal About Getting it Right When You Have To* (2010)

Brock, Timothy and Melanie Green, *Persuasion: Psychological Insights and Perspectives* (2005)

Caruso, David and Peter Salovey, *The Emotionally Intelligent Manager* (2004)

Chabris, Christopher and Daniel Simons, *The Invisible Gorilla: and Other Ways Our Intuitions Deceive Us* (2010)

Cialdini, Robert, *Influence: Science and Practice* (2009)

Darley, John, *Social Influences on Ethical Behavior in Organizations* (2001)

Dweck, Carol, *Mindset: The New Psychology of Success* (2006)

Eckman, Paul, *Telling Lies: Clues to Deceit in The Marketplace, Politics and Marriage* (2001)

Fisher, Roger and Daniel Shapiro, *Beyond Reason: Using Emotions as You Negotiate* (2005)

Hogarth, Robin, *Educating Intuition* (2001)

Kahneman, Daniel, *Thinking Fast and Slow* (2011)

Kegan, Robert and Lisa Laskow Lahey *Immunity to Change: How to Overcome It and Unlock the Potential in Yourself and Your Organization (Leadership for the Common Good)* (2009)

Knapp. Mark and Judith Hall, *Nonverbal Communication in Human Interaction* (2005)

Kiser, Randall, *Beyond Right and Wrong: The Power of Effective Decision Making for Attorneys and Clients* (2010)

Kramer, Roderick, *Social Decision Making: Social Dilemmas, Social Values and Ethical Judgments* (2009)

Krieger, Stephan and Richard Neumann, *Lawyering Skills: Interviewing, Counseling, Negotiation and Persuasive Fact Analysis* (2003)

Kupfer, Andrea and Christopher Honeyman, *The Negotiator's Fieldbook: The Desk Reference for the Experienced Negotiator* (2006)

Malhotra, Deepak and Max Bazerman, *Negotiation Genius: How to Overcome Obstacles and Achieve Brilliant Results at The Bargaining Table and Beyond* (2007)

Mayer, Richard, *Applying The Science of Learning* (2010)

McNookin, Robert and Scott Peppet, *Beyond Winning: Negotiating to Create Value in Deals and Disputes* (2000)

Nisbett, Richard and Lee Ross, *Human Inference: Strategies and Shortcomings of Social Judgment* (1980)

Nisbett, Richard and Lee Ross, *The Person and the Situation: Perspectives of Social Psychology* (1991)

Pashler, Harold, *The Psychology of Attention* (1998)

Payne, John, et al., *The Adaptive Decision Maker* (1993)

Petty, Richard and John Cacioppo, *Attitudes and Persuasion: Classic and Contemporary Approaches* (1996)

Rellis, Tamara, *Perceptions in Litigation and Mediation: Parallel Worlds of Lawyers, Plaintiffs, Defendants and Gendered Parties* (2008)

Scalia, Antonin and Bryan A. Garner, *Making Your Case: The Art of Persuading Judges* (2008)

Schacter, Daniel, *The Seven Sins of Memory: How the Mind Forgets and Remembers* (2001)

Schwartz, Barry, *The Paradox of Choice: Why More is Less* (2004)

Tavris, Carol and Elliot Aronson, *Mistakes Were Made (But Not By Me): Why We Justify Foolish Beliefs, Bad Decisions, and Hurtful Acts* (2007)

Thompson, Leigh, *The Mind and Heart of the Negotiator* (2009)

Weiner, Bernard, *Judgments of Responsibility: A Foundation for a Theory of Social Conduct* (1995)